M000187653

To put a slight riff on a [...]
somebody." Even though [...]
trust shouldn't be in our he[...]
"Dare to be a Daniel!" – you've heard it and so have I. But that
approach leads to trusting in ourself, which is far worse. Instead,
let the skillful hands and pastoral heart of Sean Lucas graciously
lead you to a different under-standing of this book and its hero,
an understanding of the mysterious and marvelous goodness of
God and grace of Christ, the true hero. That's where we can put
our trust.

STEPHEN J. NICHOLS,
Research Professor of Christianity and Culture,
Lancaster Bible College, Lancaster, Pennsylvania.

What can you expect from this book? Well, God-centered,
Christ-focused, gospel-infused exposition for starters. In addition: textually driven, careful exposition based on a belief that
every word of Scripture is Spirit-breathed; illustrative material
that opens windows to fresh air and light; and passion – that those
who read it will become aware of the riches of the gospel and the
Spirit-filled, Jesus shaped lives that ought to be the pattern of all
who, like Daniel, love the gospel and live as though they do. And
what of "the second half of the book of Daniel?" Dr Lucas, who
combines the skills of a pastor, historian, and theologian, gives
us some of his finest material. So, purchase and read, and see for
yourself what a treasure this book is.

DEREK W. H. THOMAS,
Minister of Preaching and Teaching,
First Presbyterian Church, Columbia, South Carolina.
Editorial Director, Alliance of Confessing Evangelicals.

Unique in its combination of narrative and apocalyptic style,
Daniel has intimidated many a preacher and eluded most laymen.
But Dr Lucas clarifies the big idea for all and it will preach …
God wins! Lucas the theologian, historian, preacher, pastor and
writer has gifted the Church with a study that is redemptive-

historical in its interpretation, Christ-centered in its application and enjoyable as a read.

GEORGE ROBERTSON,
Senior Pastor, First Presbyterian Church, Augusta, Georgia.

Sean Lucas' *Daniel: Trusting the True Hero* is a wonderful, engaging, God-centered treatment of the book of Daniel. His strong redemptive-historical approach keeps God's character and unfolding plan for His people central throughout. In both the narrative portions and the prophetic portions Sean helps the reader see the greatness of God and our need to trust Him in every circumstance we encounter. The focus on God as the true hero lifts the eyes of the reader beyond a great story and complicated prophecy to a personal encounter with the living God that is both accessible and devotional. I highly recommend this book for everyone from those studying Daniel for the first time to Bible study groups to long-term students of the book of Daniel.

MARK L. DALBEY,
VP of Academics & Faculty Development,
Covenant Theological Seminary, St Louis, Missouri.

Daniel

Trusting the true Hero

Sean Michael Lucas

CHRISTIAN FOCUS

Sean Michael Lucas serves as senior minister at the First Presbyterian Church (PCA), Hattiesburg, Mississippi. Prior to this, he was Chief Academic Officer and associate professor of church history at Covenant Theological Seminary, St. Louis, Missouri. He received BA and MA degrees from Bob Jones University and the PhD degree from Westminster Theological Seminary. He is the author and editor of several books, including *What is Grace?* and (co-edited with Robert Peterson) *All for Jesus*.

Unless otherwise noted, Scripture quotations are from *The Holy Bible, English Standard Version*, copyright © 2001 by Crossway Bibles, a division of Good News Publishers. Used by permission. All rights reserved.

Scripture quotations marked NIV are taken from the *Holy Bible New International-al Version*. Copyright © 1973, 1978, 1984 by International Bible Society.Used by permission of Hodder & Stoughton Publishers, a member of the Hodder Headline Group. All rights reserved. "NIV" is a registered trademark of International Bible Society. UK trademark number 1448790.

Copyright © Sean Michael Lucas 2011

ISBN 978-1-84550-732-9

Published in 2011
by
Christian Focus Publications,
Geanies House, Fearn, Ross-shire,
IV20 1TW, Scotland, UK.
www.christianfocus.com

Cover design by Daniel van Straaten

Printed by Bell & Bain, Glasgow

MIX
Paper from responsible sources
FSC® C007785

All rights reserved. No part of this publication may be reproduced, stored in a retrieval system, or transmitted, in any form, by any means, electronic, mechanical, photocopying, recording or otherwise without the prior permission of the publisher or a licence permitting restricted copying. In the U.K. such licences are issued by the Copyright Licensing Agency, Saffron House, 6-10 Kirby Street, London, EC1 8TS www.cla.co.uk.

Contents

Preface

People tend to come to the Old Testament book that Daniel wrote for two reasons. One is because they are looking for a moral example to inspire them to stand for God in a godless world. These Christians hum the chorus to the Philip Bliss hymn, "Dare to be a Daniel! Dare to stand alone! Dare to have a purpose firm! Dare to make it known!" Or maybe, if they are from my generation, it might not be Bliss's song, but the Christian musician Russ Taff's "Not Gonna Bow." Both generations' songs express the idea that the world is evil and that Christians need to be moral leaders for their generation. In order to do so, there would be no greater example or hero than Daniel.

Another reason some people study Daniel is to find out more data about the end of time. At the Christian college that I attended, the Bible class that covered Daniel paired it with the book of Revelation; clearly, the reason to study Daniel, according to the way the curriculum was developed, was to consider its prophetic materials and to understand what will happen at the end of the world. And many

Christians have spent a great deal of time thinking about Daniel 2, Daniel 7, and Daniel 9:24-27, and about how those texts fit into charts and graphs that explain the return of Christ, the tribulation, and the new heavens and earth.

However, neither reason – either moral example or biblical eschatology – is a good one for studying Daniel's book. The reason why Christians throughout the world should study Daniel's book is that Daniel teaches us a great deal about Daniel's God. As we learn the various God-centered lessons that Daniel offers, we learn to trust God as our True and Only Hero. And our heroic God is presented in the full range of his character in Daniel: we see him as faithful and wise; as a Savior and a Sovereign; a God of judgment and power; a God who rules and who orders everything for his glory; a God of forgiveness and a God who fights for us. Above all, in each chapter, we will see that our God is a God of hope.

After all, our hope is not grounded in the fact that we can dare to be like Daniel. Our hope is grounded in the character of our great God who triumphs over all his and our enemies and who orders everything for our salvation. And this God's character is displayed most clearly in his Son, Jesus, to whom Daniel, along with the rest of the Old Testament, points. As we take our hearts to the God who has come near to us in Jesus, we take our hearts to the only one who can save us, the only one who can satisfy us, the only one who can be our hero.

Thus, my prayer is that all those who study Daniel along with me will grow in faith, hope, and love as our eyes are raised to see how great and glorious and beautiful our God is.

While I consulted a number of commentaries in preparing these studies, there were two upon which I relied heavily: Tremper Longman III, *Daniel*, NIV Application Commentary (Grand Rapids: Zondervan, 1999), and George M. Schwab, *Hope in the Midst of a Hostile World: The Gospel According to Daniel* (Phillipsburg: P&R, 2006). Between the two of them, Longman and Schwab helped to shape a number of my interpretative judgments. The framing of the themes and the structure and outline of the arguments are my own.

I am grateful for the opportunity to share these studies in Daniel with a reading public. In preparing these, I am thankful for William MacKenzie and Willie MacKenzie, who each encouraged me to prepare this book for publication. Thank you, brothers, for your prayers and confidence. Gratitude should also be expressed to the congregations and groups who first heard these studies, including Covenant Presbyterian Church, St Louis, Missouri, and the First Presbyterian Church, Hattiesburg, Mississippi. I am so grateful that God has called me to serve people, both in the Midwest and deep South, who are hungry for God's Word.

The session at First Presbyterian Church, Hattiesburg, has encouraged me to write and has viewed it as part of my call in their midst. I am thankful for these dear brothers, godly men who lift me up and sustain this ministry with their prayers. The ministry staff at the church encourage and support this ministry as well: thank you, friends, for the way you love me and the way we work together for God's glory in this place. Gratitude as well should be expressed to Pat Brier, who did the initial transcription work on these chapters. And above all, I'm grateful to our congregation, who has embraced all the Lucases with its love and prayers.

I would also like to express my gratitude to the Lord for my family. My parents, Steve and Susan Lucas, and parents-in-law, Ron and Phyllis Young, continue to love us well. My wife, Sara, and children, Sam, Liz, Drew, and Ben, prod me to lift my eyes to trust in our faithful God. Though we have traveled a long journey since I first began studying Daniel, we have learned to trust this triune God as the only truly satisfying being in the entire universe. Thanks be to him above all!

1
Dare to be a Daniel?: Learning to trust a faithful God

One summer when our children were younger, our family was on a trip from St Louis, Missouri, to Atlanta, Georgia, for our denomination's General Assembly. We rarely go on such trips without allowing some time for historical explorations, and this trip was no exception. We stopped in Nashville, Tennessee, in order to visit Hermitage, the home of the seventh president of the United States, Andrew Jackson. The house and the grounds were beautiful; on the property was the Hermitage Presbyterian Church where Jackson worshiped each Lord's Day.

I was so interested in what we saw that I purchased and read the three-volume biography of Jackson written by the respected historian Robert Remini. I was particularly struck by the way Remini opened his book, attempting to justify his decision to write on Jackson. "At one time in the history of the United States, General Andrew Jackson of Tennessee was honored above all other living men. And most dead ones, too. The American people reserved to him their total love and devotion," he observed. "No American ever had so powerful an impact on the minds and spirit of his contemporaries as did Andrew Jackson. No other man ever dominated an age spanning so many decades. No one, not Washington, Jefferson, or Franklin, ever held the American people in such near-total submission." Andrew Jackson was, in Remini's memorable phrase, "the impossible Hero."

Jackson was larger than life, bigger than George Washington, an impossible hero. Americans named their children after him (as did one of my wife's ancestors and as did my wife and I at the birth of our third child). He was admired, and his life served as a grand example to a nation growing up in the wilderness. He fought against America's enemies, whether British or Indian or centralized banks. And when he died, he was memorialized in countless ways – with cities and towns and counties named after him and with his portrait on the twenty-dollar bill. All this because he was the impossible hero.

I think that is how most Christians think of the biblical character Daniel. Many of us have read something of Daniel's book. We've heard about Daniel in our vacation Bible schools and in Sunday school. We've read about Daniel to our children. We've urged people, and especially our young people, to be like Daniel. We've taught people to sing, "Dare to be a Daniel! Dare to stand alone!" In all of this, we have learned to view Daniel as an exemplary figure, someone after whom we can pattern our lives, someone who is an "impossible hero."

All of this misses the point of the book and the point of how this book functions within Holy Scripture. What we are going to discover as we consider Daniel and his book is this: the hero of Daniel's book is not Daniel, but God himself. And the big message of Daniel's stories and prophecies was not that God's people should "Dare to be a Daniel," but that they should dare to trust in Daniel's God. This

God is the true impossible hero, the one who delivers his people from all their troubles, the one who draws near in faithfulness in the worst of times.

At the point in time when Daniel's book opens, Israel probably wondered whether their God was in fact such a hero. In 605 B.C., the Lord had given Jehoiakim into the hand of the Babylonian king, Nebuchadnezzar (1:2). This was the first of three raids or sieges against Jerusalem; Nebuchadnezzar comes against Jerusalem, lays siege, takes Jehoiakim, steals some of the religious vessels, seizes some of the princes, and returns to Babylon.

Now, Israel might have been tempted to see this as the work of an evil, godless king from a far-off land. But Daniel's book stresses that this was God's work and that God was in control: "And *the Lord gave* Jehoiakim king of Judah into his hand" (1:2). After centuries, four hundred years after Solomon's reign and spiritual adultery (see 1 Kings 11:1-8), after warning Israel and Judah about their idolatry and sensuality, God finally delivered his people into the hands of their enemy. And this was the beginning of the end for Jerusalem – Nebuchadnezzar would set up Zedekiah as a puppet governor, but when the latter rebelled, the Babylonian king would finally destroy Jerusalem in 586 B.C..

Imagine Israel's reaction to exile. The holy city destroyed. The walls that were meant to protect Zion utterly obliterated. Princes taken away from Jerusalem. The sign of God's presence, the temple, leveled. As a godly Israelite living through the dark years of 605-586 B.C., one would have wondered: "Is God really there? Does God really care about us? Is he going to be faithful to us? How is God going to keep his promise to David? How is God going to bring a prophet like Moses? How will we make sacrifices that will point to a perfect priest like Aaron if the entire city is leveled and the temple is utterly destroyed?"

God's people were in exile, and they felt utterly abandoned. In our own day, we know a little of how that feels. Many of us feel as though we are strangers in a strange land; we feel as though we are "resident aliens," to use theologian Stan Hauerwas's phrase. We feel as those who are in exile from our true land, the new heavens and the new earth. As a result, we feel slightly out of joint here. We sing Zion's songs in a world that does not know Zion's God. We use time differently from the world around us; we especially delight in the Lord's Day as a day of rest and worship, not a day of personal satisfaction and recreational activities. We raise our families differently from those who do not know the true and living God. We work in our callings differently than others; we know that our work is a gift given to us by God to bring him praise, not an idol meant to satisfy our hearts. We live out of joint with our times; we live as though we're in exile, as though we are resident aliens.

And yet, living as exiles in a strange land is difficult. It is hard to always feel out of step with the people around us; it is difficult never to feel at home. In those times where the grind of being exiles wears us down, we are tempted to ask, "Is God really there? Is God faithful? Is he going to keep his promises?" And that's where Daniel's message meets us: the God we worship is the true hero. He is a God who is truly faithful, not only for people two thousand years ago or four thousand years ago, but for us today. He is a God who comes near to us in our desperate need and says again and again, "I am the True King; I will be faithful to you. I will keep my promises because I love you. And I showed you my love pre-eminently by pursuing you all the way to the cross and to the empty tomb in Jesus Christ."

As we trust in this God, we find hope as resident aliens, as exiles living in a strange land.

A faithful God put to the test
We learn to trust our God as we pay attention to this man, Daniel. It is hard for us to approach this book because it is so familiar to us. And this is especially the case with this story in Daniel 1. How many times have we heard about Daniel and his friends and their challenge? And yet, we must slow down and pay attention to the text once again, asking God to let us hear it with the freshness that Israel would have known when they first read Daniel's book.

The first thing we discover is that Daniel and his three friends were youths, but they were more than that: they were royal princes (1:3-4). In an effort to secure the loyalty of far-flung peoples and the unity of a vast empire, Nebuchadnezzar brought royal princes from the various conquered peoples in order to re-educate them. And so, that's who Daniel was. He was a prince, one of the royal sons. Perhaps he was part of the family that would ultimately produce the Messiah. And he came to Babylon for re-education: he learned the literature and language of the Chaldeans (1:4). He received a new name (1:7). He gained "learning and skill in all literature and wisdom;" in fact, it appears that the four young men learned Babylonian divination as well (1:17). Even more, not only did Daniel learn, he excelled in all that the Babylonians taught (1:20). It doesn't appear that Daniel was begrudgingly submitting to this re-education process; rather, he embraced it fully and was excelling.

And yet, he objected at the point of the food. Why? Why did Daniel resolve that he would not "defile himself with the king's food, or with the wine that he drank" (1:8)? We have to say first what this was not: this was not a brief for vegetarianism. Daniel was not a vegan; he was not saying that he only wanted to eat kosher. Rather, Daniel and his friends were determined to demonstrate and maintain their utter reliance upon their God. If they succeeded, they did not want the credit to go to Nebuchadnezzar, and especially not to Nebuchadnezzar's god. If they succeeded, all credit would go to Yahweh, Israel's covenant-making, covenant-keeping God, the God who would remain faithful even to exiles in a foreign land.

And so, in order to demonstrate this, they proposed the test: "Test your servants for ten days; let us be given vegetables to eat and water to drink. Then let our appearance and the appearance of the youths who eat the king's food be observed by you, and deal with your servants according to what you see" (1:12-13). Ashpenaz, the king's steward, listened to them and agreed. At the end of the ten days, "they were better in appearance and fatter in flesh than all the youths who ate the king's food" (1:15). The test succeeded; Daniel and his friends no longer have to eat the king's food and so "defile themselves."

But we have to say that the test didn't succeed because of the vegetables and the water. In fact, the test wasn't about the food at all. *The test was about the faithfulness of Daniel's God.* It was Daniel's God who intervened in such a way to show that in fact *he* was the faithful God, the one who keeps covenant and who will remain faithful to Israel even in exile. He was the one who would sustain their bodies, who would give them learning, who would prosper them in the foreign land. And the big point here, flashing so brightly that Israel could not miss it, was this: while the Babylonians may want to believe they are in charge, that they are the true kings of the world, that they are the ones ruling over a vast empire, the fact is that Israel's God is actually in charge. He was the one who sent Israel into exile.

He was the one who continues to be present with Israel in exile. He was the one who will make them a blessing in exile. And he was the one who will sustain Israel (pictured in Daniel) all the way to the reign of King Cyrus of Persia – the foreign ruler whom Israel knew would deliver them and bring them back home (1:21; see Isa. 45-47).

What Israel and we need to hear
Indeed, Israel needed to hear that God would be faithful all the way to their deliverance. Israel did not need to hear that vegetables and water would preserve them; rather, they needed to hear that God would be faithful. Just as God was faithful to Daniel, so by extension God would be faithful to Israel. Even though they were in exile, even though the temple was destroyed, even though the wall was knocked down, even though it was not clear how the Davidic line would continue – despite all of this, Yahweh was still in charge, still faithful, still remembering his covenant.

That's what we need to hear. As dark providences come to us and as we experience struggle, we need to know that God is still faithful. As we get the call from a loved one who gives us horrible news; as the doctor comes into the room and tells us that it's cancer; as we stand by the graveside of a child, wondering where God is – whatever it may be, in the dark providences of our lives, when we feel as though all of life is swirling around, when we feel that we are in exile from God and from our true home, we need to hear and know that God is faithful. Even far from the land of promise, God is there. And the words of William Cowper's hymn come to teach us that

> *God moves in a mysterious way his wonders to perform;*
> *He plants his footsteps in the sea, and rides upon the storm.*
> *Deep in unfathomable mines of never-failing skill,*

17

He treasures up his bright designs, and works his sovereign will.
Judge not the Lord by feeble sense, but trust him for his grace;
Behind a frowning providence he hides a smiling face.

We don't understand sometimes – as we wander through this wilderness land, in exile from our true home, living as strangers and aliens, we confess that we don't know why things happen or why evil seems so strong. But we do believe that in those times, our God is actually as near to us as our breath; he is at our right hand, holding it, leading us through the storm. And we must learn what Israel needed to learn from Daniel – God the King is faithful. He has not abandoned us.

A blessing even in exile

Not only did Israel need to hear that God would be faithful, but they also needed to know that God wanted them to continue to be a blessing even in Babylon. The striking thing about Daniel's test is how successful it was and how successful God was in the midst of it. We see this particularly in Daniel 1:19-20. Daniel and his three friends finally came to the end of their three-year training period. Along with hundreds, perhaps thousands of others, they stood before Nebuchadnezzar for their oral examinations. Can you imagine how intimidating that would be? What would be the unthinkable consequences of failing such an examination? And yet, Daniel and his friends didn't fail; in fact, "among all of them none was found like Daniel, Hananiah, Mishael, and Azariah ... . And in every matter of wisdom and understanding about which the king inquired of them, he found them ten times better than all the magicians and enchanters that were in all his kingdom" (1:19-20).

Now, why was that important? It was important not simply for Daniel and his friends to be in a high position;

rather, Israel needed to hear that Daniel and his friends were present in Babylon to be a blessing. In part, this was a fulfillment of God's promise to Abraham a thousand years prior to Daniel. In Genesis 12, God appeared to Abraham and promised, "I will bless those who bless you, and him who dishonors you I will curse, and in you all the families of the earth shall be blessed" (Gen. 12:3). That promise was still in play even though it looked like the Promised Land was gone and even though it looked like the promised seed would not come. Israel was still called to be a blessing. The prophet Jeremiah had tried to tell them this as they went into exile. He had said, "Seek the welfare of the city where I have sent you into exile, and pray to the LORD on its behalf, for in its welfare you will find your welfare" (Jer. 29:7). Israel needed to hear that as they went into exile into Babylon, they were there to be a blessing.

That's what God calls us to do. Here in our place of exile, in this place where we sometimes feel out of joint and out of step with our culture, God calls us to be a blessing. We're not here to transform our culture (we can't), but we're here to be a blessing to others in real and tangible ways. Whether it is assisting poor and disadvantaged children in reading programs, whether it is writing notes to those struggling with cancer, whether it is participating in civic leadership – whatever it may be, God has called us as a people in exile to be a blessing to our host culture. There are countless ways that God may be calling us to be a blessing to someone whom we run across, but the fact remains that God still desires to bless his world and to bless people who do not know him. And he wants to bless them through us.

Real defilement
But Israel needed to hear a third message, perhaps the most important message of the chapter. God was telling Israel here:

"Though you may gain the learning of Babylon, though you may eat the food of Babylon, though you may bear the names of Babylon (1:7, 11, 19), don't defile yourself."

But there is a problem in the way we have heard this in the numerous times we've come to this text. Some of us think that the defilement could come through the food; others of us think that the defilement could come through the learning. But God doesn't put the defilement in either of those places. Where does the defilement come from? Where did it come from for Israel for hundreds and hundreds and hundreds of years prior to this scene? Defilement comes from a heart that does not honor Yahweh alone as the true God of the world.

Why was Israel in exile after all? Because they worshiped idols and called them Yahweh – the sin of the golden calf and ultimately of Jeroboam (Exod. 32; 1 Kings 12:25-33). And then, far worse, they worshiped other gods and abandoned the worship of Yahweh completely (2 Kings 21:1-18). And from where did this idolatry come? It came from their hearts; it was their hearts that presented the problem. As Jesus said, "Out of the heart come evil thoughts, murder, adultery, sexual immorality, theft, false witness, slander. These are what defile a person" (Matt. 15:19-20). All defiling sin and idolatry comes from the heart.

And that's the problem; it is my sinful heart and your sinful heart. Our sin is real and deep and deceptive and pervasive. Day after day, we defile ourselves by not trusting God to be faithful in a variety of situations. We don't seek the Lord's face when we're confronted by a variety of decisions. Instead, we trust the idols of our own hearts: we trust ourselves, our own wisdom, our strength, our smarts. And in doing so, we defile ourselves, we compromise, and we fail to be a blessing as exiles in a hostile world.

Though that seems like bad news, it actually is good news. Because as those who falter and fail, who struggle and sin, who love our idols and our host culture more than our God and our true home, we need someone who is truly exemplary, who is a true hero, who can deliver us from our defilement and our sin. And that is ultimately why God tells us about Daniel. Because in showing us a man like Daniel, who was willing to trust his faithful God in the face of a hostile culture, God actually points us to one beyond Daniel, who not only is faithful to the end in the face of a hostile world, but also came to deliver us from our ultimate alienation and exile.

Trusting Jesus, the Faithful Savior

In other words, Daniel teaches us to look to Jesus. Though we were wandering far from God, in exile and alienation from him, Jesus came to bring us near to God. In doing so, he showed us that God was ultimately faithful all the way to the cross. In addition, in Jesus Christ, we are enabled and empowered to be a blessing to others. We are granted the Holy Spirit so that we might live in ways that are not native to us, that are not natural to us. We can put off the old man and put on the new man. We can move truths from our heads to our hearts. Why? Because in Jesus Christ we have been granted the Holy Spirit to empower us. And by the Spirit of Jesus, we are empowered and enabled to be a blessing without compromise. As our hearts delight in our union and communion with Jesus, we experience the total devotion to God for which we are made and of which the First Commandment speaks. And yet, in those moments when we falter and fail, when we are defiled, we can come again and again to Jesus and find fresh forgiveness and renewed mercy.

Thus, as we come to Daniel and this wonderful first chapter, we discover that God is not calling us to "Dare to be a Daniel." Instead, we hear "Dare to Trust Jesus" and live for his glory, not because we have the native strength to do it, but rather because Jesus makes it possible by granting us the power that comes from God alone. In this way, we discover that even when we are unfaithful, God remains faithful, and we learn to trust this faithful God as an exiled people on our way home.

FOR FURTHER REFLECTION

1. Think about someone you know who seems "heroic." What makes them a hero? How do these qualities reflect God's character?

2. Why is it so difficult for us to trust that God will be faithful? When dark providences enter our lives, why do we struggle to see "God's smiling face"?

3. What does it feel like to be an exile or a resident alien? In what ways is that a helpful image for living as a Christian today? How might we think about Christian calling in fresh ways as a result?

2
God only Wise: Learning to trust a wise God

Have you ever had a strange dream that you couldn't forget? Or maybe it was a nightmare that came over and over again? One such dream that I remember from when I was a kid was a recurring nightmare in which I was in an abandoned house, being chased by the members of the 1970s rock band KISS. It was very, very strange; band member Gene Simmons, in particular, has always creeped me out. I would wake up in cold sweats from those nightmares.

A couple of years ago, I had another recurring nightmare. When I served at Covenant Presbyterian Church in St Louis, I felt the stress of preaching and leading the church as interim minister while also working at Covenant Theological Seminary as dean of faculty. At the time, I was preaching through Psalms; in my dream, I stood in the pulpit, and everyone was looking at me. I said, "Turn in your Bibles to the book of Psalms," but when I turned to where the Psalms were supposed to be, they weren't there. I kept looking and looking, but I never found Psalms. That was terrible.

As adults, we are used to having these dreams and often wonder what our dreams tell us. In fact, even if we aren't Freudian, we probably believe that our dreams are the working out of repressed emotions or the result of profound stress. Even more, we look to our dreams to tell us things because, as human beings, we are on a constant search for wisdom and insight into our worlds and ourselves. We want to know how we work, how things work, and how to make our way through life successfully.

We want to know these things because life often seems shrouded in mystery. We apply for jobs for which we believe we are qualified and we don't get them. We wonder why; it seems to be a dark mystery. What happened? Why didn't I get that job? We work our way in the corporate world and we get crosswise with our boss or a co-worker. We don't understand; every time we open our mouths it seems to make things worse. And we wonder, is all this my fault? How in the world is this happening to me?

Above all, we wonder why the wicked prosper, why power and influence appear to follow some for a time. We read the gossip columns and the "everyday" sections in our newspapers, aghast at the lifestyles of the rich and famous, the powerful and admired – and we wonder whether their lives represent the real wisdom in this world. After all, some of us can't make ends meet and can't move through life in a way that incurs less pain; but the movie stars and politicians and Wall Street barons seem to move through life with all that they need and desire. Maybe their lives represent true wisdom. Maybe our lives are less than that.

Certainly, God's people in every generation have had every reason to think this, every reason to believe that those who lived by power and might, sensuality and idolatry, were the truly wise ones. The time described in Daniel

2 saw Israel in exile, crushed by the might and power of an evil nation, Babylon. Not only were God's people crushed, they were taken into a foreign land to serve a pagan people who had apparently used their idols to triumph over Yahweh, Israel's covenant God. And God's people must have thought: "What is going on here? Didn't God promise to protect us as his people? Didn't God promise to establish David's son as king forever? Doesn't God love us? Does God still care?"

Even more, Israel had every right to ask the question: who was truly wise? Those who follow the gods of the Babylonians? Or those who follow Yahweh, Israel's covenant-making, covenant-keeping God? And sometimes, we ask these questions – we wonder whether those who follow the gods of this world are really the wise ones after all.

That's why this chapter was so important in the message that Daniel had for God's people. This chapter was meant to show Israel – and ultimately us – that our God, the God of Israel and the church, is not only faithful, but is also the only wise God. Babylon's magicians couldn't come through because Babylon's gods couldn't come through. Only Yahweh could. Only our God, the God who has come near to us in Jesus Christ, only *this* God could come through with wisdom, power, might, and glory.

Unmasking all pretensions

The way God demonstrated that he was superior to all false gods was to unmask the pretensions of Babylon's gods. I say "unmask" because this chapter presents a scene that is, at one level, tragicomic. Nebuchadnezzar, the powerful ruler of Babylon, puts his magicians in a terrible spot, an impossible situation. We discover as the text opens that the king has had a dream. This dream was produced by more than psychological distress or repressed emotion. This dream was a revelation from God, a message to the king about the future.

When the king awoke, he demanded that his magicians not only interpret the dream, but tell it to him as well. When the magicians asked the king to tell them the dream, he threatened them: "The word from me is firm: if you do not make known to me the dream and its interpretation, you shall be torn limb from limb, and your houses shall be laid in ruins" (2:5).

As the magicians gulped, they again appealed to the king to tell them the dream. And again, they got a forceful response: "I know with certainty that you are trying to gain time, because you see that the word from me is firm – if you do not make the dream known to me, there is but one sentence for you. You have agreed to speak lying and corrupt words before me till the times change. Therefore tell me the dream, and I shall know that you can show me its interpretation" (2:8-9). Essentially, Nebuchadnezzar was saying, "You think you can just keep lying to me and telling me what I want to hear. You think that you can play it safe until somebody assassinates me and takes control of this kingdom. Well, I'm not going to put up with it. And that's why I'm putting you to the test. And if you can't comply, you die."

In reply, the magicians set the stage for the rest of the scene: "There is not a man on earth who can meet the king's demand ... the thing that the king asks is difficult, and no one can show it to the king except the gods" (2:10-11). Whether the magicians had darker motives or not, they made it plain that they couldn't give the king what he wanted. They were brought to an end and, by implication, their gods were as well. Neither the magicians nor the gods could give the king the answer that he desired. Naturally, this wasn't good enough for the king – and so, he orders all the wise men to be killed. As far as the wise men were concerned, it would take a miracle for something or someone to intervene.

When the captain of the king's guard came to arrest Daniel and his friends, Daniel spoke to him with "wisdom and tact" (2:14 NIV). Already it was clear that Daniel was a genuinely wise man, a sage. But the reason Daniel was so wise was revealed in what happens next: he went to his friends and told them "to seek mercy from the God of heaven concerning this mystery, so that Daniel and his companions might not be destroyed with the rest of the wise men of Babylon" (2:18).

These men went to God with this matter, praying for mercy. In response to their prayer, God revealed the "mystery" to Daniel in a vision of the night. And when Daniel praised God, he declared, "Blessed be the name of God forever and ever, *to whom belong wisdom and might ... he gives wisdom* to the wise and knowledge to those who have understanding; he reveals deep and hidden things; he knows what is in the darkness, and the light dwells with him. To you, O God of my fathers, I give thanks and praise, for *you have given me wisdom* and might, and have now made known to me what we asked of you, for you have made known to us the king's matter" (2:20-23, emphasis mine).

Notice how Daniel, in his praise of God, contrasted his God with the false gods of Babylon. First, the Babylonian magicians had claimed that only the gods could give that answer; by implication, they didn't expect that to happen (2:10). By contrast, Daniel sang that his God, the God of Israel, had all "wisdom and might" (2:20).

Moreover, Nebuchadnezzar was concerned that the magicians were lying in wait "till the times change" (2:9), until they could topple him from power and secure the kingdom for themselves. By contrast, Daniel sang that his

God, the God of Israel, "changes times and seasons; he removes kings and sets up kings" (2:21).

In addition, the Babylonian magicians operated with their divination, their "dark arts," their false worship. By contrast, Daniel worshiped a God who "reveals deep and hidden things; he knows what is in the darkness, and the light dwells with him" (2:22). Against Babylon's gods and magicians, Daniel sang to his God as the only truly wise God: "you have given me wisdom and might" (2:23). The pretensions of Babylon's gods and Babylon's wisdom were completely unmasked because Daniel's God was the only wise God.

And so, Daniel came before the king to reveal and interpret his dream for him. When confronting the king, Daniel made the point of telling him that "there is a God in heaven who reveals mysteries, and he has made known to King Nebuchadnezzar what will be in the latter days" (2:28). Not because of "any wisdom that I have more than all the living" (2:30), but because Daniel's God was the true God – he was the one from whom wisdom came. The dream centered on a strange statue, the appearance of which was "frightening" (2:31). It was made of gold, silver, bronze, iron, and clay. Then the king saw a large boulder, "cut out by no human hand" (2:34), which struck the feet and toppled the statue. The wind carried away the pieces of the statue "so that not a trace of them could be found." But the boulder "became a great mountain and filled the whole earth" (2:35).

Daniel's interpretation must have assured the king, for he told him that "you are the head of gold" (2:38). After Nebuchadnezzar, kingdoms of lesser and mixed qualities would arise. At some point, "the God of heaven will set up a kingdom that shall never be destroyed, nor shall the kingdom be left to another people. It shall break in pieces all these kingdoms and bring them to an end, and it shall stand forever" (2:44).

Now, there has been a great deal of discussion over two and half millennia about what these metals stood for. The traditional interpretation is that they represent Babylon, Medo-Persia, Greece, and Rome. But it strikes me that which kingdoms are represented is far less important than two important truths: first, God is in control of human history. God was the one who told this pagan king what human history will be. How does God know these things? He knows it because he has foreordained it, he has purposed it, he has determined it. He is the grand conductor of human history, and his wisdom is what ultimately stands.

There is a second important truth: God's own kingdom will ultimately supplant all human kingdoms. In the days of all those kings, the God of heaven will establish another kingdom that will never be destroyed, nor will it be left to another people. It will break into pieces all human kingdoms and bring them all to an end. And God's kingdom will stand forever, filling the entire earth.

And that, of course, is what happened. If the traditional interpretation is correct, then we can say that Babylon, Medo-Persia, Greece, and Rome no longer exist as powers. And even the contemporary kingdoms of this world – United Kingdom, the United States, China – they will all pass away. But on a hill called Golgotha, God established his reign in Jesus' death; and on the third day, he vindicated his King as the True King over the world. And King Jesus is subjecting every enemy to himself until the day comes when sin and death, the world and the devil, shall be no more (1 Cor. 15:20-28; Heb. 2:5-9). He is establishing his reign, and when he is done, God will be all in all.

Notice the king's response: it is striking – the king of the entire known world fell on his face prostrate before an exiled Jew. And he acknowledged that Daniel's God was far superior to all Babylonian gods because "you have been able to reveal this mystery" (2:47). And in the same way, all the kings of this world at the end of the age will lie prostrate at the feet of a crucified Jew (Phil. 2:9-11). They will praise our God as "God of gods and Lord of kings," far superior to all their idols of false religion and statecraft. And they will admit his wisdom and their own folly to his eternal glory.

Hope for a foolish people

This story must have given Israel great hope. They must have recognized that their God had triumphed over the Babylonian gods, undoing all their pretensions. But they also must have seen their own foolishness.

After all, why were Israel and Judah in exile? Because of their idolatry. Repeatedly, God had come to Israel and Judah through his prophets and remonstrated with them, urging them to repent and to turn back to him as the great lover of his people. They had thought that the nations around them were so wise for worshiping the Baals and Dagons, engaging in gross sexual practice and in the horrendous cult of child sacrifice. What had that gotten Israel and Judah? Exile. Why? Because those gods weren't so wise after all; Israel was in fact worshiping "the works of their own hands" and had become dumb just like their idols (Jer. 1:16).

Yet, God in his mercy and his steadfast love comes again to his people to woo them. He demonstrates that he is the only wise God, the only one who can reveal deep and hidden things, the only one who can see in the darkness. That truth should have brought hope and given comfort to God's people.

And that should give hope and comfort to us as well. As God's people, we must cling to this truth: our God knows what's in the darkness. He knows the path we tread. He's able to see in those dark places in our lives. There are so many times as we walk along the path of life, with its twists and its turns, that we would give anything to know what's on the other side, but we can't see that far. We seem to be stumbling along in the darkness, but God sees in the darkness. He reveals deep and hidden things; he knows what's in the darkness and the light dwells with him. And he's able to shine his light so that we can see what the next steps might be.

Why is he able to do this? Because he alone is the wise God. He alone is the king of the universe. In fact, his wisdom and might are tied together in this text twice: "Blessed be the name of God forever and ever, to whom belong *wisdom and might*" (2:20); "To you, O God of my fathers, I give thanks and praise, for you have given me *wisdom and might*" (2:23). We confess these grand theological truths: that God is wise and that God is sovereign; that God looks through time and history and knows the future because he foreordained it to happen; he is omnipotent and powerful. We confess these truths, but it is in the darkness of our lives that we find that we come to believe them, we come to stake our entire futures on those grand truths.

And that means we stake our lives on the fact that God is greater than all his and our enemies. He was greater than Nebuchadnezzar, though that king ruled the entire known world. He was greater than the magicians, who claimed to be able to discern all mysteries. He is greater than your sickness, your losses, your depression, your fear, your doubts. He is greater and more powerful, able to intervene and to do all that he purposes to do.

What Daniel's story calls for us to do, along with God's ancient people, is to believe, to trust him, not to doubt or to fear, but to know that our God is one "to whom belong wisdom and might." That is why we sing these words from "Guide Me, O Thou Great Jehovah:"

> *Open now the crystal fountain, whence the healing*
> *   stream doth flow;*
> *Let the fire and cloudy pillar lead me all my journey*
> *   through.*
> *Strong deliverer, strong deliverer, be thou still my*
> *   strength and shield.*

Our God is a strong deliverer, leading us through this barren land. And he calls on us to trust his leading, even as dark providences and painful moments enter our lives.

Indeed, he invites us, along with Israel, to call out to him. That's the turning point in this story, when Daniel and his companions do not rest in their own wisdom, but rather turn their hearts to rest in the wisdom of God: "Daniel went to his house and made the matter known to Hananiah, Mishael, and Azariah, his companions, and told them to seek mercy from the God of heaven" (2:17-18).

This is so difficult for us. I have a friend who, whenever I talk to him and I am dealing with anything sticky or complex, will stop me and say, "I'm glad to help you, Sean, but wait a second, let's pray about this first." Why is it that our hearts have such a difficult time turning to call out to this God? In this account of the only wise God we should see the true solution to our darkness. In our times of darkness and struggle, we must recognize that God is taking us to the place where we come to the very end of ourselves so that we will have nowhere else to turn. And he does that so we will turn to him and pray to him for his mercy, wisdom, and might. That is the best place for us, because such is the place of our weakness and God's power.

The way the Wise King works for His Kingdom

God also brings us to this place because this is the way Jesus the King works in order to establish his kingdom. Remember, there was a larger point here in this vision. The point was not simply that God was the True King of Israel in the midst of their exile. Rather, the point was that God the True King was going to deliver his people and ultimately establish a kingdom that would never fail.

We know from the rest of the story of the Bible that God does exactly this. In Jesus' death, burial and resurrection, God in Jesus has inaugurated his rule over this world. Jesus is establishing a kingdom that is a great rock, a boulder that will fill and encompass the entire world. Those are real promises: God is working so that the glory of the knowledge of God will cover the world as the waters cover the seas (Isa. 11:9). And every knee will bow; and every tongue will confess that Jesus Christ is Lord to the glory of God the Father (Phil. 2:10-11). While we may not see everything in subjection to Jesus yet, we do see Jesus who has given himself for sinners like us (Heb. 2:5-9). And this glorious King strengthens us by his Spirit and calls us to engage this world and see the hints of his reign being made manifest in the lives of families throughout our neighborhoods, cities, and world.

Because, after all, God already knows the entire story. He knows it from beginning to end. He knows that, at the end of human history, all things will be made new, and King Jesus will wipe away every tear from every eye. And he shall be all in all. Ultimately, as we live our lives here, sometimes we feel disjointed with our world, sometimes we feel as though we are in exile, sometimes we walk through the darkness, sometimes we struggle. But we take great comfort in the fact that the King we serve is the God of gods and Lord of kings. He is the only wise God, and we delight to worship him and him alone.

FOR FURTHER REFLECTION

1. Remember a recurring dream you have had. Did you obsess about what the dream meant? Why? How might that make you sympathetic to Nebuchadnezzar's situation? In what ways might your own obsessing about your dream's meaning signal a longing for divine wisdom?

2. Have you been tempted to believe that the contemporary idols of our culture represent true wisdom for life? How does Daniel 2 serve to overturn that temptation?

3. In what ways does this chapter of Daniel offer hope? Make a list of these and consider how you might live more faithfully today as a result.

3

The Fiery Furnace: Learning to trust a Savior God

We love rescue stories. Whether it is a movie such as *Saving Private Ryan* or a great 1980s television show like *MacGyver*, we love watching heroes who are able to escape from all kinds of scrapes and difficult situations in order to rescue another. For some of us, we enjoy reading books where the hero is able to work his way through a knotty problem in order to rescue another: Sherlock Holmes, one of my personal favorites, was excellent at this. Holmes could put together the most obscure facts in order to solve the mystery and rescue his client from harm. We love stories where there are rescues involved and mysteries resolved.

And preferably, these rescues come near the end of the story. We don't want the story to drag on into multiple volumes or several sequels of a movie. Except for the hit television show *Lost*, where the rescue came at the end of the sixth season, we want deliverance or a rescue then and there. That's what makes such stories so great: the deliverance comes and all is put back to order again in the world.

What gives Daniel 3 such power is that it is a rescue story. But what also gives it such power is that while the reader knows the end of the story, we recall that the three friends – Shadrach, Meshach, and Abednego – did not know how this would all play out. As likely as not, they were thinking that they would not be delivered. And that's what gives this story its power: the wonder of what they are doing is their ability to trust God even while they are experiencing a fiery trial.

This trust in God in the midst of difficulty, opposition, persecution, and suffering was something that Israel needed to see. It is also something that we need to see and hear and believe. Because the fact of the matter is that we go through difficulties, affliction, opposition, and persecution; we know what "fiery trials" feel like and look like (1 Pet. 1:6-7). As we are in the midst of these trials and in the testing of our faith that they offer, we need to know and believe that the God whom we serve, the God of Israel and the church, the God who has come near in Jesus, is able to save us out of the trial. But not only this: we must also believe that our Savior God comes near to us in the midst of the trial and walks through it with us.

The model: Daniel's friends

In the previous chapter, Nebuchadnezzar had dreamed of a huge statue: its head was made of gold, the chest of silver, and the lower half of bronze, clay, and iron. At some point – we aren't sure when – the king decided to make a ridiculously huge statue – approximately 90 feet high and 9 feet wide. It was made completely out of gold. He set this golden statue up in a level place ("the plain of Dura," 3:1) near the royal city of Babylon and demanded that it be worshiped.

Why did Nebuchadnezzar do this? Again, we're not exactly sure. Perhaps he took this idea from his dream. After all, the head of gold represented him and his kingdom; perhaps he began with this image and decided to expand on it. We're not sure whether this statue was a representation of Nebuchadnezzar himself or whether it was meant to represent one of his deities. What is important to recognize, however, was that this represented Nebuchadnezzar's great feat; it was a sign of his power to build a statue of gold so large; and it was admission of his godlike status to bow down to the statue at his command. And in a real way, this was the most dangerous kind of idolatry: an idolatry stripped of religion, an idolatry of power, self, and pride, attributing sovereignty to forces and persons other than the true God of the world.

And yet, though Nebuchadnezzar was able to demand worship, he wasn't able to convert people's hearts. In fact, the rhythms of the text suggest the mindlessness and monotony of the entire scene – over and over again, the officials are listed (3:2-3, 27); over and over again, the instruments are listed (3:4-5, 7, 10, 15). And, seemingly, everyone in the entire world ("all the peoples, nations, and languages," 3:4, 7) – except the three friends – mindlessly bows down. The people bow down, but they can't believe that this was anything but yet another ruler engaged in yet another self-aggrandizing act. And so, they go along to get along: "Give the king your body, but keep your heart for yourself."

Nebuchadnezzar apparently didn't notice that there were three, out of the entire empire, who did not bow down. It took several Babylonians to accuse them before the king. It seems, at least from 3:12, that these men were jealous of the three friends' positions: the men described them as the "certain Jews whom you have appointed over the affairs of the province of Babylon." And these Jews, these exiles, these outsiders, "pay no attention to you" (3:12).

If there were words that were calculated to get Nebuchadnezzar's attention, those would be the words. Basically, these Babylonian officials were hitting the king right at the heart of the issue: "These men are not like us; they don't believe that you are the true king of the world; they don't believe that you are godlike." It's no wonder that Nebuchad-nezzar flew into a "furious rage" (3:13); these three friends had challenged his pretensions to be godlike and all-power-ful. That could not be: and so, he had the friends arrested and brought before him. He gave them a choice: they could either bow down and worship the image or they could be immediately cast into a "burning fiery furnace" (3:15). But most telling were his final words: the king in his anger, in his supposed power as a godlike emperor, boasted, "And who is the god who will deliver you out of my hands?" (3:15).

Shadrach, Meshach, and Abednego felt no need to defend themselves, but they did testify to their covenant-making, covenant-keeping God. "Our God whom we serve is able to deliver us from the burning fiery furnace, and he will deliver us out of your hand, O king. But if not, be it known to you, O king, that we will not serve your gods or worship the golden image that you have set up" (3:17-18).

With these words, the three friends acknowledged both the reality of God's power and the mystery of God's pur-poses. God is able to deliver: the God who created all things by the power of his word could certainly intervene in this moment. But God may not deliver for reasons that seem best to him: for he is the God who not only created out of his power, but also out of his wisdom (Prov. 8:22-31). They did not presume that God would, in fact, rescue them; they admitted that they could die. But they also confessed their determination to pay more attention to their God, the True King of the world, than the king who was pretending to be the true god of the world.

Not unexpectedly, Nebuchadnezzar didn't like this answer: he "was filled with fury and the expression of his face was changed" against the friends (3:19). He became so hot that he decided to make the furnace even hotter: "He ordered the furnace heated seven times more than it was usually heated" (3:19). It is so hot that the men who had bound the friends and who threw them in the fire died from the heat. There's no doubt that the king expected the friends to die a similar death.

But two amazing things happened. First, the friends were unharmed, unbound, and "walking in the midst of the fire" (3:25). How does *that* happen? But second, there was a fourth person in their midst, and his appearance "is like a son of the gods" (3:25).

And so, Nebuchadnezzar inches up to the furnace. He can't get too close because it is still so hot, but he comes close enough to shout, "Shadrach, Meshach, and Abednego, servants of the Most High God, come out, and come here!" (3:26). Here is the first indication that the king is beginning to realize that another God, far more powerful than him, was at work: he admits that these friends are servants of "the Most High God."

But he has further confirmation when the friends emerge. As he and the mindless officials who had bowed down to his great feat examined the friends, they saw that "the fire had not had any power over the bodies of those men. The hair of their heads was not singed, their cloaks were not harmed, and no smell of fire had come upon them" (3:27). This was truly amazing: not a hair on their heads had been harmed (cf. Matt. 10:30; Luke 21:18), but even more, they didn't even smell like smoke! Those of us who have roasted marshmallows over an open fire or grilled out hamburgers know how impossible this is. Here was rescue and deliverance in the first degree! This was a miracle! This was God entering in and delivering Shadrach, Meshach, and Abednego.

The king was humbled and confessed that Israel's God, the God whom Daniel and his friends trusted, had rescued them. He even professed admiration for these friends who "set aside the king's command, and yielded up their bodies rather than serve and worship any god except their own God" (3:28). For, clearly, "there is no other god who is able to rescue in this way" (3:29). Catch that? No other god: not Nebuchadnezzar and not his gods. Whose God? Shadrach, Meshach, and Abednego's God: *this* God was able to deliver out of the king of the world's hand and rescue his own.

The message to Israel: comfort

Now surely, this message should have comforted Israel. They were in exile; the holy city had been destroyed; the Davidic princes had been taken into exile. God had told Israel through the prophet Jeremiah that they would be in exile for seventy years, and maybe longer – as far as the people were concerned, who knew if Jeremiah got it right? God's people felt as though they were in a "fiery furnace": opposition, persecution, affliction, and suffering. In fact, the teachers were probably recalling the words of Deuteronomy 4:20 for the people: "The LORD has taken you and brought you out of the iron furnace, out of Egypt, to be a people of his own inheritance, as you are this day." Egypt was once the fiery furnace; now Babylon was. When would God come and deliver his people again? When would God come to deliver out of the fiery furnace?

And in answer to these questions, God's people heard this story of Daniel's friends being delivered from the fiery furnace by the direct intervention of their God. Their response should have led them to confess that God had the power and ability to rescue them, to save them from exile, and to restore them once again to a position of prominence in the world.

But the comfort didn't simply come from the fact that God *could* rescue; rather, there was comfort in the fact that God *came down* to rescue. He came down into the fiery furnace, and he would come down to rescue them once again.

That's a good word not just for Daniel's time but also for our own. We might be going through a fiery trial right now: persecution, opposition, affliction, suffering. God's Word tells us that this will happen: "Beloved, do not be surprised at the fiery trial when it comes upon you to test you, as though something strange were happening to you" (1 Pet. 4:12). Some may be experiencing "insult for the name of Christ," genuine suffering as a Christian (1 Pet. 4:14, 16). Others may be struggling deeply with dark emotions – with anger, shame, lust, or fear. Still others may be dealing with a besetting sin and wonder if they will be delivered, whether God has the power and ability to rescue. We confess that these trials knock us off our feet; they cause us to lie in bed with our chest pounding, our hands sweating, our mind racing.

God's Word speaks to us in the midst of our fiery trials and calls us to trust in our God because he is powerful. Our God, the God we know as Father, Son, and Spirit, is able to enter into our struggle and deliver us. He is able to enter into situations that appear impossible to us – fiery trials that would kill other men and women – and he is able to rescue. We learn to trust the power of our God and we know merciful comfort.

We also learn to trust the promises of God. We know Scriptures such as 1 Corinthians 10:13: "No temptation has overtaken you that is not common to man. God is faithful, and he will not let you be tempted beyond your ability, but with the temptation he will also provide the way of escape, that you may be able to endure it." We remember places such as Isaiah 43:2-3: "When you pass through the waters, I will be with you; and through the rivers, they shall not overwhelm you; when you walk through the fire you shall not be burned, and the flame shall not consume you. For I am the LORD your God, the Holy One of Israel, your Savior." God's promises comfort us as we learn to trust his power in the midst of our struggles.

But above all, we look to the Resurrection of Jesus. We see the empty tomb, we hear the angels say that "He has risen; he is not here" (Mark 16:6), and we believe that the God who raised Jesus from the dead – an apparent impossibility – can enter into our own suffering and struggle and impossibility and create life out of death. Because we trust in the God who has come near to us in Jesus, the Resurrection and the Life, we believe that God can enter into our struggle. We believe and are comforted.

The message to Israel: confront
And yet, while this story was a comfort to Israel, it would have confronted them as well. First, Israel would have been confronted by the fact that faith doesn't demand that God rescue. Rather, faith trusts that God is able to rescue, and if God chooses not to rescue us, he will work even this for our salvation. In other words, Israel was confronted by the mystery of God's purposes along with the reality of his power.

Of course, this was seen most clearly in the response of the three friends: our God is able to rescue us, they said, and he will. But even if he does not, we will still trust in him. And in this response, we see that the story doesn't hold out the false promise that God will save every faithful person from suffering and death. The mystery of God's purposes means that we often don't know the greater purpose that God may have in our struggle and suffering.

And so, we learn to repeat and rest in the wonderful words of the first answer in the sixteenth-century Heidelberg Catechism:

My only comfort is that I am not my own, but belong — body and soul, in life and in death — to my faithful savior Jesus Christ ... He also watches over me in such a way that not a hair can fall from my head without the will of my Father in heaven; in fact, all things must work together for my salvation.

We must admit that sometimes it is the will of our heavenly Father that we go through dark providences and painful times. And yet, we also believe that behind this dark, frowning providence, behind this dark cloud, there is a smiling face, though we cannot and may not see it for months or even years. We also confess that God does not bring these fiery trials into our lives because he's angry with us or because he desires to punish us or harm us. No! Our God desires to draw us closer to him even through the painful and fiery trials we experience.

John Newton expressed this well in one hymn text:

I asked the Lord that I might grow
in faith, and love, and every grace;
Might more of his salvation know
and seek, more earnestly, his face.

'Twas he who taught me thus to pray,
and he, I trust, has answered prayer!
But it has been in such a way,
as almost drove me to despair ...

Yea, more, with his own hand he seemed
Intent to aggravate my woe;
Crossed all the fair designs I schemed,
Blasted my gourds and laid me low.

"Lord, why is this," I trembling cried;
"Wilt thou pursue thy worm to death?"
"'Tis in this way," the Lord replied,
"I answer prayer for grace and faith."

"These inward trials I employ,
from self and pride to set thee free
and break thy schemes of earthly joy,
that thou may'st find thy all in me."

God often employs fiery furnaces in our lives in order to break us from our own idolatry of self and pride in order to draw us nearer to him.

But there is a second lesson that should have confronted Israel: idols cannot rescue or deliver us; only the true and living God can. Remember why the Israelites were in exile. They weren't in exile because they needed a vacation from Palestine; they were in exile because of their idolatry. They were in exile because they did not really believe that Yahweh was as good as he said he was; they did not believe that his steadfast love was in fact better than life. Rather, they looked to the gods of the other nations, worshiping them, clinging to them, offering sacrifices and even their own children to them. And God brought judgment upon them in order to shake them from their idolatry: the northern kingdom smashed by the Assyrians, the southern kingdom by the Babylonians.

And so, during this time of exile, God's people needed to learn the hard lesson that the idols of the Babylonians and Philistines and Assyrians and Egyptians and Persians could not save them. Only their God, Yahweh, the God we name as Father, Son, and Spirit – only *this* God can save them.

This same lesson is what we need to learn as well. Our idols of power and sensuality, fame and reputation, security and significance cannot save us. Academic prestige, career advancement, or community reputation cannot rescue us. Addictive idolatries to alcohol, tobacco, drugs, or sex cannot deliver us. None of these things can save us from guilt, shame, anger, or frustration. None of these things can rescue us from emptiness and abandonment. None can deliver from persecution, opposition, or affliction. Our idols cannot save us; only God can save us.

The Messiah: Jesus

Only God can save us because, in Jesus the Messiah, he came into the midst of our trial, into the midst of our fiery furnace. Remember that Nebuchadnezzar looked up and saw this fourth individual walking in the midst of the fire, and he said that he looked like a "son of the gods" (3:25). The Son of God, whom we know as Jesus the Messiah, in fact walked among us. He experienced our pain, suffering, and even death itself. God's Word tells us that "he offered up prayers and supplications, with loud cries and tears, to him who was able to save him from death" (Heb. 5:7). God is powerful, and he was able to save Jesus from death.

But in the mystery of God's own purpose, he didn't. Rather, he allowed Jesus to die, experience godforsakenness, and to bear the fiery trial of separation from God as the sin-bearer. And because he entered into our suffering as the Messiah, the one who came to "save his people from their sins" (Matt. 1:21), he is able to sympathize with us in our sorrows and sustain us to the end (Heb. 2:17-18, 4:15-16). He speaks to us by his Word and Spirit and says softly,

> *When through fiery trials your pathway shall lie,*
> *My grace, all-sufficient, shall be your supply;*
> *The flame shall not hurt you; I only design*
> *Your dross to consume and your gold to refine.*
>
> *The soul that on Jesus has leaned for repose,*
> *I will not, I will not desert to his foes;*
> *That soul, though all hell should endeavor to shake,*
> *I'll never, no never, no never forsake.*

As we wrestle with our trials, with exile, persecution, opposition, and affliction, God calls out to us to trust in him. He shouts to us to trust that he is a Savior God, one who is able to save, one who entered into our suffering to rescue. He doesn't promise to save us *from* the fire; but he does promise to save us *in* the fire. We can trust that he will never forsake us, not now, nor at the end of the age.

FOR FURTHER REFLECTION

1. Consider your life over the past six months. Has there been a fiery trial that has nearly overwhelmed you? What has your response been?

2. In what ways does Daniel 3 comfort you? Why should your hope increase because you know that God came down to rescue the three friends? What would it look like for God to come down into your situation?

3. In what ways does Daniel 3 confront you? Are you tempted to trust in other deliverers? To demand that God rescue?

4
The King of the World: Learning to trust a Sovereign God

It had been a brutal night for the champ, Sonny Liston, that day in late February in 1964. His opponent, a 22-year-old heavyweight named Cassius Clay, had cut him under his right eye in the third round. For three additional rounds at the old Miami Convention Hall, Clay kept jabbing and jabbing at Sonny Liston's right eye; not only had Clay hurt Liston, but he was leading on all the judges' scorecards. It wasn't supposed to be this way. Clay, 1960 Olympic gold medal winner in the heavyweight division, was a 7-1 underdog; Liston had been confident going into the fight that he wasn't going to lose.

But as the bell rang for the seventh round, Liston didn't budge from his stool. When the referee instructed him to come out of his corner, Liston refused, complaining of a separated shoulder. Cassius Clay – 7-1 underdog, a boxer we know better by the name Muhammad Ali – became the heavyweight champion of the world. And while we may not remember many of these details, most probably have seen Ali's reaction to his victory. Once Liston was counted out, Ali began to run around the ring and shout at the television camera, "I'm the greatest! I'm the greatest thing that ever lived! I'm the king of the world!"

We know that our athletes tend to exaggerate their importance; when they do, we smile a little bit at the braggadocio that drives them to do amazing feats. But when other powers, other forces, other circumstances scream out to us, "I'm the king of your world," suddenly we smile no longer. Instead, we know the anxiety, fear, and dismay that come from someone or something else claiming to be king over our lives and our world.

For some, it is in the workplace. Our bosses demand the impossible workweek, week after week; they demand a ridiculous travel schedule that takes us away from our family, our church, our lives; and they implicitly threaten us that if we refuse to do this, we'll lose our jobs. In doing this, our bosses act as though they are the true kings of our world.

For others, it's an illness. Our child is in the hospital, connected to tubes and wires and monitors. We hear the doctor's diagnosis and prognosis; fear and anxiety are the result, dominating our days, turning our weeks into a death march. And in the midst of these terrors, we begin to wonder whether sickness is, in fact, the king of our world.

For still others of us, the devil himself opposes and accuses us. He knows that particular weak point, that particular sin with which we wrestle and struggle, sometimes successfully and sometimes not so successfully. As he points, prods, and tempts us so that we falter and fail over and over again, we begin to think that the devil himself is the true king of our world.

And death itself can seem this way. As we lose a loved one to death or as we struggle ourselves, standing with one foot in the grave, we begin to fear. We wonder whether Jesus will actually receive us into the Celestial City; our hearts begin to falter and fail. And we begin to wonder whether death itself is the true king of the world.

These powers, forces, circumstances, and spiritual opponents are very real. Let's make that clear: the pain, fear, and anxiety that we often feel, the thought that these things are ultimate reality, challenge us to the core of our being. We can't rationalize them away or minimize these things. Our hearts cry out, "Are these things ultimate reality? Are these powers, forces, circumstances king? Or is there another outside of us who is the true king of the world?"

Certainly, Israel knew what this felt like. For them, there was a great and mighty power, Babylon, headed by a king who truly was the king of the known world. At one point, Nebuchadnezzar ruled the territory from the border of modern-day Iran west through Iraq; north through modern-day Turkey and south through Palestine to Egypt. This one man ruled most of the known world stretching from the Mediterranean Sea to the Persian Gulf for forty-three years.

Moreover, this mighty power ruled by this impressive king was utterly pagan. In Israel's eyes, Nebuchadnezzar and the Babylonians were violent, vicious idolaters; they represented wickedness and evil to the godly believers of Zion; they were the uncircumcised who did not know or obey the law of God. And yet this pagan king destroyed Israel's Davidic king, the Holy City, and the Holy Temple. In doing so, it appeared that Nebuchadnezzar's triumph was not only over Israel's rulers; it appeared that his triumph was over Israel's God. Israel wondered, "Is Nebuchadnezzar really the king of the world? Is there another king, a True King, who is able to triumph over him, to humble and even humiliate him?"

With these questions in mind, the words of Daniel 4 must have trumped all of Israel's expectations. In this chapter, we have a royal encyclical from the pagan king who utterly destroyed Israel, took them into exile, and worshiped his pagan deities in which he admits that he is not in fact the true king of the world. Rather, he acknowledges that the God of Israel and the church is King, the one whom we know as the God revealed in our Lord Jesus Christ.

The humbling of Nebuchadnezzar

From the opening of our text, we hear this strange hymn of praise, a testimony to the "signs and wonders of the Most High God": "how great are his signs, how mighty his wonders! His kingdom is an everlasting kingdom, and his dominion endures from generation to generation" (4:2-3). But don't miss this: these words are not coming from Israel's King David, Solomon, Josiah, or Hezekiah. *Nebuchadnezzar* declares these words "to all peoples, nations, and languages, that dwell in all the earth" (4:1). The pagan king had come to bow the knee to Israel's God, and he did so by singing this hymn of praise.

Now, careful readers of Daniel to this point should expect that Israel's God would be shown as a powerful king, but the way it happened surprises and confounds us. The way it happened moves us from Nebuchadnezzar's strange hymn to his strange dream. Once again, as in Daniel 2, Nebuchadnezzar had a dream (4:5); once again, he brought in all the wise men of Babylon (4:6-7); once again, he had to get Daniel to come and interpret the dream (4:8).

When Daniel came to hear the dream, he discovered that it centered on a large tree that "grew and became strong" (4:11), with its top in the heavens and its visibility extending throughout the earth. Perhaps this was like an ancient Near Eastern ziggurat, a tower of worship that reached to the heavens; we aren't sure. But it is clear that it dominated the landscape in a way similar to the "great feat" of Daniel 3, the golden statue that could be seen from miles around. In the vision, the birds lived in the tree; the beasts lived under it. But then, there was a voice that cried out, "Chop down the tree and lop off its branches, strip off its leaves and scatter its fruit" (4:14) – only a stump remained. And words of judgment were declared: "Let him be wet with the dew of heaven. Let his portion be with the beasts in the grass of the earth. Let his mind be changed from a man's, and let a beast's mind be given to him; and let seven periods of time pass over him" (4:15-16).

In response to this dream, Daniel was "dismayed" and "alarmed" (4:19) – he knew that this meant judgment from God. The tree was Nebuchadnezzar; he was the one "who [has] grown and become strong. Your greatness has grown and reaches to heaven, and your dominion to the ends of the earth" (4:22). But the decree of heaven was that Nebuchadnezzar was to be driven away from humankind and become like an animal. Why? What was the purpose in this judgment? That "you [may] know that the Most High rules the kingdom of men and gives it to whom he will" (4:25). Essentially, God told Nebuchadnezzar, "You think that you're the true king of the world, but you must know that Heaven rules. You are not the true king; once you acknowledge the True King, then you will know sanity once again."

It was a strange dream with a strange meaning. But evidently, Nebuchadnezzar forgot about it, because a year later, everything happened just as God had said. One night, Nebuchadnezzar was walking on the roof of his palace, perhaps admiring the hanging gardens, perhaps admiring the great architectural feats. And he said to himself, "Is not this great Babylon, which I have built by my mighty power as a royal residence and for the glory of my majesty?" (4:30). When considered in the bright light of day, it was a crazy thing to say: to claim that he was godlike and that Babylon was for the glory of his majesty. But immediately, "while the words were still in the king's mouth," the voice from heaven shouted in judgment (4:31). He lost his sanity, was driven from among men, and ate grass like an ox.

Nebuchadnezzar continued in this condition until he finally "lifted [his] eyes to heaven" in acknowledgment of the True King of heaven (4:34). His sanity was restored; and the first thing he did was "praise and honor him who lives forever." He sang a song of praise to Israel's God, especially highlighting the true rule, the real kingship, of that God:

> *His dominion is an everlasting dominion, and his kingdom endures from generation to generation; all the inhabitants of the earth are accounted as nothing, and he does according to his will among the host of heaven and among the inhabitants of the earth; and none can stay his hand or say to him, "What have you done?" (34–35)*

These words weren't from Isaiah, David, Jeremiah, or Moses. These words were from a pagan king, one who thought he was the true king of the world. Be sure to get this: this is a pagan king who had slaughtered Israelites, leveled Jerusalem, destroyed the temple, made eunuchs of the descendants of David. *This* was the one who acknowledged, indeed, *praised* God as the True King. This would be the equivalent of the modern-day G-8 leaders, the heads of state for the Western powers, falling on their faces before God and singing a hymn of praise to the triune God, saying that he is the True King over all things. It would be stunning.

The Comforting Hope of Israel

How would Israel have heard this royal encyclical from a pagan king? What lessons would Israel have taken from this? First, Israel should have gained comfort from Nebu-chadnezzar's hymn, which confirmed the message that Daniel's book had already given: despite appearances, Isra-el's God is in control; he is the True King of the world.

Think about how hard that message was to believe for a godly Israelite. He was living in Babylon, far away from the holy city, his true home, Zion. Like the Psalmist in Psalm 73, he looked around and saw the "arrogant" and "wicked" Babylonians prospering, with "fat and sleek" bodies, proud, malicious, and mocking God. It appeared that these wicked Babylonians were prospering and that God's people were forsaken. He had to think: "all in vain have I kept my heart clean and washed my hands in inno-cence" (Ps. 73:13). To hear that God was still in control and was the True King of the world must have been difficult to believe.

Sometimes, it is difficult for us to believe. We look around us and see those who mock God prospering: pow-erful, influential, ruling, and lording it over us. We strug-gle in jobs that we don't like or for which we are ill-fitted; we wonder how long we can hold on till retirement; and we wonder where God is in the midst of it all. We wrestle with sickness and illness that leave us debilitated much of the time. We come up to the very edge of death ourselves, or we have a loved one who dies. All these things domi-nate our mental and emotional landscape; the very appear-ance of them causes us to question the message that Daniel through Nebuchadnezzar's encyclical was giving. How could it be possible that God is in control? How could it be possible that God is the True King of the world when all this evil is happening to us?

But then Nebuchadnezzar's words come to us with renewed force to comfort us: "His dominion is *everlasting*; he *does* according to his will among the host of heaven; *none* can stay his hand." This is our God he is talking about. If we doubt the goodness and power of God, then we must hear these words again: God has not abandoned us or his world. He is powerful to save and to deliver. And he will move heaven and earth to be with us, to draw near, and to rescue.

Sickness can't stop him; the devil can't stop him; the world can't stop him; death itself can't stop him – our God will draw near to comfort our hearts. Whatever circumstances, power, or forces we face, we can trust that our God rules over it for our good and his glory. He is the True King of the world. That's how it is possible to learn to sing in faith:

> *Whate'er my God ordains is right:*
> *Though now this cup, in drinking,*
> *May bitter seem to my faint heart,*
> *I take it, all unshrinking.*
> *My God is true; each morn anew*
> *Sweet comfort yet shall fill my heart,*
> *And pain and sorrow shall depart.*

We know what it is like to drink bitter cups; and yet, because our God is King, he is also true and trustworthy. He rules over every circumstance for his glory and our good; he does so because he is the King.

A word of rebuke for Israel

And yet these words of comfort also contain a rebuke. For how often do we turn our hearts away from the true and living God to chase after idols of our own devising? And so, to show us our foolish hearts once again, God brings us to situations that clearly show us our impotency. He will bring us to the end of ourselves to humble us, going to tremendous lengths to drive all our idols from our hearts so that we will turn once again to him.

In our pride, we believe that we have the resources to stand, to deliver ourselves, to solve our own problems, and to save ourselves. We try to tackle our marriage problems as though simply another book, conference, or technique can straighten things out. We seek to engage our children who are drifting away from us with toys, trips, and pleasure, thinking that there must be some parenting book somewhere to help us. We think that everyone calming down can simply solve relational problems at work. And in the end, we think that our spouses, children, and co-workers should simply agree with us because we are godlike. In those times, we act like Nebuchadnezzar. We think that we are like gods, powerful to rescue, able to save. Because we are often so hugely successful, we believe that we can work all the angles and so save ourselves.

But God will not let us go on that way. Rather, he wants us to learn from Nebuchadnezzar that he will humble us for our good and his glory. He even opposes us so that we might be humbled. And if God can humble Nebuchadnezzar, and if God can humble Israel and Judah, then he can certainly humble us. But he humbles us not because he hates us, but because he loves us and longs for us to have and know his grace: for "God opposes the proud but gives grace to the humble" (1 Pet. 5:5).

In fact, it is at that very place where we have no other place to turn that God meets us. It is when we are willing to lift our eyes to the heavens, to acknowledge the goodness and power of God, that God moves heaven and earth for us. That's why Peter calls us to "humble yourselves, therefore, under the mighty hand of God so that at the proper time he may exalt you, casting all your anxieties on him, because he cares for you" (1 Pet. 5:6-7).

So, the question we have to ask is, "Why do we fight it?" Why do we stubbornly try to save ourselves, rescue ourselves, and make ourselves godlike? Why do we not embrace the humbling that God brings to us? What we must see is that the wonder of the gospel is that God actually uses our humiliation to grant us grace and to bring him glory.

The humiliation of Jesus

How do we know this is the case? How do we know that God is able to use our humiliation for his glory and for our good? We know because we know Jesus.

As humiliating as it was for the king of the world to become a beast, to crawl around on the ground with claws and dew for seven years, Jesus knew far greater humiliation. The Westminster Shorter Catechism puts it this way: Jesus' humiliation "consisted in his being born, and that in a low condition, made under the law, undergoing the miseries of this life, the wrath of God, and the cursed death of the cross; in being buried, and continuing under the power of death for a time" (SC 27).

Think of it – the True King of the world, the one "in the form of God," with all the glory and power and might and dominion, condescended to be born (Phil. 2:6). He was born and placed in a feeding trough in a stable. He was born to a stonemason living in a forgotten town, on the backside of a mountain, called Nazareth. And not only born, but born *poor*, a servant, a tradesman – the God of heaven this is! And for thirty-three years, he underwent life's struggle – going hungry sometimes, opposed, tired. For thirty of those years, he was his father's apprentice; for the last three, he walked the entire length of Palestine, from the northernmost point where the original twelve tribes held possession to the southern tip. He was betrayed, abandoned, lonely – a man of sorrows acquainted with grief.

And the chief humiliation: the Lord of Glory, the King of Creation, the Sovereign of Life *died*. He not only died;

he bore the full wrath of his Father. He didn't die like one of the thieves on either side of him; he died like no one else could or would. He bore God's wrath, he knew godforsakenness, not for himself, but for his own people. He knew the mocking of his own creation; he made those men and women who shouted insults at him! And he was buried in a tomb – the one who was the Word and who spoke life into existence, the one who was Life itself, continued under death's power for three days.

This is far greater humiliation than Nebuchadnezzar's, far greater than anything we could know. Now the question comes: was God still in control over Jesus' life and death? Was God able to use Jesus' humiliation for his glory and power? Yes! God raised him from the dead by the word of his power and highly exalted him and bestowed on him the name that is above every name. And one day at the end of the age, every knee shall bow to the one who is the True King of the entire world, declaring that Jesus Christ is King, is Lord, to the glory of God the Father (Phil. 2:10-11).

And so, how do we know that God can intervene and rescue? How do we know that God is still King even when the world, sin, death, and the devil all appear to be in charge? How do we know that even our humiliation will work for God's glory and our good? How do we know? Because we know Jesus, the True King of the world – and because we know him, having been united to him by faith, we have a glorious promise of resurrection. But even more, because we know him, we confess that Jesus is the greatest, the greatest one who has ever lived. He is the King of the world!

FOR FURTHER REFLECTION

1. As you look at your life, who are the people or what are the events that are making the claim that they are the true kings of your world?

2. In what ways should God's ability to humble Nebuchadnezzar comfort you? Even in times when it is difficult to believe, how does God's control over all things in your life give you hope?

3. List the ways that you pretend to be the true king of your world. How does this chapter of Daniel stand as a rebuke to your pretensions?

5

Handwriting on the Wall: Learning to trust a God of judgment

There is a famous story told about St Patrick, the fifth-century missionary to Ireland. One year, the night before Easter happened to coincide with a major pagan festival that was being held on the hill of Tara in Ireland. In defiance of pagan tradition, Patrick lit a bonfire in the distance against the tribal ruler's order. This ruler, whose name was Loiguire, was incensed. "Who is it that has dared to commit this crime in my kingdom?" he shouted. "He must die!" Loiguire sent several druids to seize Patrick and bring him before the king.

When Patrick came before the king, he did not come penitent. Rather, the story claims that he summoned the power of God to raise one of the druids into the air and then release him. After that, he called for darkness and an earthquake, which killed fifty of Loiguire's men. But still the king wouldn't let him go.

The next morning, Easter Sunday, Patrick was brought back and challenged by a druid to a wonder-working battle. First, the druid made snow fall waist-deep, but Patrick made it disappear. The druid made fog appear over the land, but Patrick made that disappear as well. Finally, Patrick prayed and set the druid on fire. That made Loiguire especially furious, and he began to take steps to have Patrick punished. But the missionary stopped him, saying, "If you do not believe now, you will die on the spot; for the wrath of God descends on your head." The king stopped in his tracks. "It is better for me to believe than to die," he reasoned. Clearly, Patrick has some ability to call divine power and judgment down upon his enemies. And so, apparently, Loiguire believed that day and turned to the eternal Lord God; a number of his tribe believed as well.

Now, this is a legend, and yet we can certainly put ourselves in the position of Loiguire, the tribal king. If we saw someone who was able to cause another person to levitate, who had the power then to smash his head on the rock, who was able to have snow or fog go away on command and set people on fire, we would probably take him seriously. And if this person then said, "If you don't believe in my God and the power of my God, then God's wrath and judgment will come upon you," we would probably take that claim seriously as well. Like the king, we would be wise to reason that the wrath of God was something of which we wanted no part.

But that is what makes the scene in Daniel 5 so strange – Belshazzar had seen the power of God expressed in judgment. He was alive when his grandfather, Nebuchadnezzar, was driven from his throne through his loss of reason and then restored to his throne. One would think that he would take heed and humble himself before God. Instead, Belshazzar was revealed to be a proud, arrogant, and unrepentant man.

We get a hint that this chapter both connects and contrasts with the prior chapter in the last verse of Daniel 4:

"all his works are right and his ways are just; *and those who walk in pride he is able to humble*" (4:37, emphasis mine). That verse serves as a hinge between the two scenes – whereas Nebuchadnezzar's pride was humbled and led to the acknowledgment that God is the True King, Belshazzar's pride and arrogance allowed no other possible result but the judgment and wrath of God.

The other connecting point between chapters 4 and 5 is the way the scenes from Nebuchadnezzar's humbling are recounted in this chapter. In Daniel 5:20-21, Daniel recounts what happened to Belshazzar's grandfather, how God judged his pride and arrogance and humbled him: "But when his heart was lifted up and his spirit was hardened so that he dealt proudly, he was brought down from his kingly throne, and his glory was taken from him. He was driven from among the children of mankind, and his mind was made like that of a beast, and his dwelling was with the wild donkeys. He was fed grass like an ox, and his body was wet with the dew of heaven, until he knew that the Most High God rules the kingdom of mankind and sets over it whom he will." Belshazzar knew all of this, knew that God humbled his proud ancestor; and yet, he continued on in arrogance. And the result was the judgment and wrath of God.

The judgment and wrath of God – this is not the typical place we go in order to find hope. And yet, this text is shot through with hope for God's people. Here's why: believing that God is a judge who will set the world to rights again is profoundly hopeful. Imagine living in a world where evil is not punished. Imagine living in a world in which justice is not administered. Imagine living in a world in which crime is not punished. Murder goes unpunished; rape goes unpunished; violent abuse goes unpunished; embezzlement goes unpunished. Who would want to live in a world where there is no justice?

None of us would. That's why it is hopeful to believe that God is going to set the world to rights again. We're hardwired for justice; buried deep within our hearts as human beings is a longing for all to be set to rights, for the world to be the way it ought to be. Even in our popular culture, we find this. Recall the popular country song by Toby Keith where the chorus declares, "Justice is the one thing you should always find." We are hardwired to believe that the world ought to be just; there ought to be punishment for wrongdoers.

But such a longing for justice raises a troubling question: what about *our* sins? What about *our* crimes? What about *our* injustice? Our innate sense of justice recognizes that God's justice and wrath should come upon us as well. The Psalmist knew this: "If you, O LORD, should mark iniquities, O Lord, who could stand?" (Ps. 130:3). The fact of the matter is that we are proud, arrogant, sinful, ungodly rebels who violate God's will and deserve his wrath.

What we find in Daniel 5 is that God's justice and wrath does and will come. God will set the world, our world, to rights once again; justice will be the one thing that we will find. But as those who trust in the God who has come near in Jesus, we find hope in the fact that God judged the world of his chosen ones in Jesus. He doesn't pour out his wrath and justice upon us; rather, he took the steps necessary to bear the wrath himself. And those who are humbled and who look in repentant faith to God through Jesus find great hope – because we become part of God's purpose of making the world the way it was supposed to be all along.

An arrogant King

It is striking that the first words after the end of chapter 4, "those who walk in pride he is able to humble," are these: "King Belshazzar made a great feast for a thousand of his lords and drank wine in front of the thousand." That transition not only connected humiliation with Belshazzar, preparing us to read about this, but it also introduced a new character into Daniel's story.

Belshazzar was the son of Nebuchadnezzar's successor, Nabonidus. He served as co-regent with his father, who was in exile from Babylon. This night of feasting was actually October 11, 539 B.C.; it was the night before the Medo-Persian army broke through the walls to capture Babylon. What was Belshazzar doing then? Surely he knew that the Medes and Persians were encamped outside; surely he heard them pounding his walls and gates. Why was he drinking and feasting, rather than preparing for a final battle? We aren't exactly sure: perhaps he was trying to rally and encourage his leaders; perhaps he was giving an emotional diversion before the final onslaught; or perhaps he was confessing that resistance was futile and it was better to eat and get drunk before one died.

While we don't know why Belshazzar was eating and drinking on this night of all nights, we can imagine that this was a tension-filled feast. This was the last night of the Babylonian empire; the last night to try to placate the gods and to secure the empire for the future. As part of this process, Belshazzar commanded that the holy vessels from Israel's temple be brought out. And for whatever reason, he decided that the party should drink from these goblets and toast their gods with them. Not only did Belshazzar commit blasphemy and idolatry in doing this, he was clearly challenging Israel's God, spitting in God's eye as it were.

Why was he doing this? It stemmed from his pride and arrogance. Here was a man who ruled the largest empire known to human beings at that point. He believed that he was invincible, that he was bulletproof. Even though the Medes and Persians were camped on his doorstep, he was sitting there getting drunk with his lords. And he was using Israel's holy things to worship "the gods of gold and silver, bronze, iron, wood, and stone" (5:4).

God's response was quick. Immediately, human fingers appeared and wrote on the plaster of the wall, near a lamp stand where it could be seen. Belshazzar saw the hand and lost control of all his bodily functions: he was scared to death (5:6). Here was a sign that was verifiable; everyone could see this handwriting on the wall. Unsure of what the words meant, he gathered together all the magicians, Chaldeans, enchanters: but they couldn't interpret the writing. That frightened him again: the gods (or God) had spoken, and he didn't know what the words meant.

Finally, the queen mother showed up. This was perhaps Nebuchadnezzar's wife, perhaps Belshazzar's stepmother of sorts, someone who had married Nebuchadnezzar but who was not Belshazzar's own mother or grandmother. While her exact relationship to Belshazzar was unclear, her love for his grandfather was very clear. There was a bit of a needle in her words in Daniel 5:11: "In the days of *your father*, light and understanding and wisdom like the wisdom of the gods were found in him, and King Nebuchadnezzar, *your father* – *your father* the king – made him chief of the magicians, enchanters, Chaldeans, and astrologers" (emphasis mine). Three times she makes reference to his ancestor, Nebuchadnezzar (calling him his "father"): perhaps she was highlighting the wisdom of Nebuchadnezzar against the folly of Belshazzar; perhaps she was noting the halcyon days of the past against the coming days of doom.

In any event, the queen mother reminded him of Daniel, who had been highly regarded by the previous regime. He had been part of Nebuchadnezzar's inner circle – he was "chief of the magicians" (4:9) – but had been displaced from that position. At this point, Belshazzar viewed him with disdain; when Daniel was finally brought to him, Belshazzar arrogantly referred to him as "one of the exiles of Judah" of whose reputation he had "heard" (5:13-14). But he still doubted whether Daniel could help him: "If you can read the writing and make known to me its interpretation ..." (5:16). His pride and arrogance were astonishing; surely he was aware *who* Daniel was and more importantly *whom* Daniel served. For one whose color changed in fear at the sight of God's hand, he seemed quite recovered in his arrogance.

The response from Daniel was not good; essentially, Daniel told Belshazzar that he had not been paying attention. He recounted the scenes of Daniel 4, but then reminded Belshazzar that he knew all this: "And you his son, Belshazzar, have not humbled your heart, though you knew all this, but you have lifted up yourself against the Lord of heaven" (5:22-23). In his pride and arrogance, he not only disbelieved Daniel, but even more, he had disbelieved Daniel's God: "the God in whose hand is your breath, and whose are all your ways, you have not honored" (5:23).

And because Belshazzar was proud and arrogant and because he would not humble himself before the Most High God, judgment was coming: God had numbered the days of the kingdom and brought it to an end; he had weighed the king and found him wanting; and the kingdom would be divided and handed over to the Medes and Persians. And that very night, Belshazzar was killed; an army led by Darius, the lead general sent by the Persian king Cyrus, captured Babylon. And the words came true: "those who walk in pride he is able to humble" (4:37).

The Almighty's justice
Imagine how Israel would have heard this story. After all, one of the songs in their hymnbook was Psalm 137. This

song had been written during their time in exile in Babylon. And it expresses a longing for God's justice that is palpable and real:

> *By the waters of Babylon, there we sat down and wept, when we remembered Zion. On the willows there we hung up our lyres. For there our captors required of us songs, and our tormentors, mirth, saying, "Sing us one of the songs of Zion!" How shall we sing the Lord's song in a foreign land? ...O daughter of Babylon, doomed to be destroyed, blessed shall he be who repays you with what you have done to us! Blessed shall he be who takes your little ones and dashes them against the rock! (Ps. 137:1-4, 8-9).*

We recoil at this. We wonder what in the world this is doing in our Bibles. But what we should see here is not Jewish-Babylonian hatred. Rather, what we should see in Psalm 137 is a deep and profound longing for justice, a longing for God to exercise vengeance, a desire for God to set things to rights.

Understand what happened through your imaginations; don't sanitize the effect of Nebuchadnezzar's destruction of Israel. Nebuchadnezzar killed *fifty thousand* Jews. He leveled Jerusalem. He burnt the temple, the most holy place imaginable. His men raped women, murdered children, and slaughtered defenseless people. His siege led to horrible acts of degradation, including cannibalism and the eating of feces. And what made all this even more horrifying was that these Babylonians were pagans. They claimed that their god, Marduk, had triumphed over Yahweh; the wicked were punishing the righteous, the lawless destroying those who had God's most holy law. And so, when Israel sang Psalm 137, they were not expressing ethnic hatred. They were longing for God to be righteous, for God not to let the criminals get away with what they've done, for

God not to let those who commit such atrocities triumph. They were longing for judgment, justice, and wrath as part of the world's being set back to order once again.

We know what this feels like. Americans can remember back to 9/11, to the day when terrorists slammed two jetliners filled with people into New York City's World Trade Center, and one Boeing 737 into the Pentagon. The desire for vengeance, justice, and wrath against those who perpetrated these attacks was nearly universal in the United States. President George W. Bush related this in his memoir: as he walked through the rubble of the World Trade Center three days after the attack and tried to comfort people, he found that comfort was not what they wanted. One firefighter looked him square in the eye and said, "George, find the bastards who did this and kill them." Regardless of whether or not one agrees with the way the United States did this, the main point is this: when we experience injustice, even atrocities, we long for vengeance, revenge, justice. This was exactly what God's people felt in Psalm 137, all the way to longing for someone to take Babylonian babies and smash their heads against the rocks. And so, when Darius the Mede showed up on Babylon's doorstep, God's people believed that here was justice at last. Here was one small step toward setting the world back to rights, to the way it ought to be.

Of course, it was one small step because there are so many things about our world and ourselves that are not the way they ought to be. We see the effects of sin and injustice all around us, and we cry out, "Lord, set the world to rights again; take vengeance; execute judgment; bring this to the right conclusion." We have things like this in our lives all the time. When we've been sued on grounds that are utterly frivolous and yet involve us in lawsuits that take years to resolve themselves, we long for justice to come.

When we've been ripped off in a transaction and there's no recourse, no way to somehow get our money back, we long for justice to come. When we drink water that's unclean or breathe air that's dirty or fear to go outside because of the criminal actions of others, we long for justice to come. When our spouse who stood before God and witnesses walks away and ceases to keep his or her promises, we long for the world to be set to rights. When we bear the marks of abuse, by the hand or the word of another, we long for the world to be set to rights again.

These things scream out to us, "The world is not the way it ought to be yet!" All things are not yet in subjection to Jesus; we know this. But our hearts still question, "Is anyone going to deal with this? Is God going to deal with this? Does he even care?"

Daniel 5 tells us God cares. God is going to set things to rights. There is coming a day when God will execute judgment. Those who have sinned and executed crimes and have not received justice will receive it in the end. We can believe this because God is a God who sets things to rights again. God is a God whose very character demands that his creation be put back into order. He will answer our constant prayer for things on earth to be done as they are in heaven.

And yet, the promise of final judgment and of a final setting to rights of all accounts should cause a shudder to pass through us. After all, what was justice to Belshazzar only came after decades of justice to God's people. It was just for them to be in exile and captivity. They had been idolaters, blasphemers, and adulterers; their exile was divine punishment, justice, and wrath. And this reality points us to our own sin, our own injustice, our own transgression and iniquities. In those secret places of our hearts and minds are sins of pride and arrogance, blasphemy and idolatry, sensuality and murder, lying and covetousness. If God were to judge us right now as we are in ourselves, we would be undone, for we are a people of unclean lips, hearts, and minds. Is there any hope for us? Is there any way for God to forgive us so that we do not have to bear the wrath, justice, and vengeance we deserve?

The Atoning Sacrifice of Jesus

The good news of the gospel is that we have hope. And we have hope that God will not stand against us as a judge but will turn to us the face of a loving father, because he has poured out his justice and wrath on Jesus Christ. That is our hope. That is why we sing:

> *How deep the Father's love for us, how vast beyond all measure*
> *That he should give his only Son to make a wretch his treasure.*
> *How great the pain of searing loss — the Father turns his face away*
> *As wounds which mar the Chosen One bring many sons to glory.*

We sing this because the good news declares to us that on the cross, Jesus bore the full wrath and judgment of God. Not for himself and not for his sins, but he bore this judgment for our sins, for the sins of all his people. God's Word tells us that God put Jesus forward "as a propitiation by his blood" (Rom. 3:25), an atoning sacrifice that satisfied God's wrath against us.

Even more, through the death of Jesus, God demonstrates to a watching world his determination to set the world to rights again. As the Apostle Paul puts it in Romans 3:26: "It was to show his righteousness at the present time, so that he might be just and the justifier of the one who has faith in Jesus." God displays to the world that he takes sin as an affront to his infinite honor and dignity; hence, sin is an infinitely heinous crime that deserves eternal judgment and wrath. But God's justice is satisfied through the death of Jesus, the infinite Son of God. And for all those who come to him through Jesus, he declares, "Right with me!" God sees us in Jesus and sees us as having already borne his justice in him. He grants and credits to us the perfect satisfaction, righteousness, and holiness of Jesus! All our sin, injustice, evil, horror – all gone: as if I had never sinned nor been a sinner, as if I had been as perfectly obedient as Christ was obedient for me!

And at the cross, through Jesus, God has already begun to set the world to rights. He has already judged sin and injustice, death and the devil. He has taken our enemy and crushed his head on Golgotha's Rock! He is "o'er every foe victorious!" And so it is, in the great truth that God is a judge, we find hope. For we believe that God has judged our sin at the cross of Jesus and views us as part of the world as it one day will be again. In us, he is displaying to the entire world what it looks like when he puts things back to rights!

FOR FURTHER REFLECTION

1. In our contemporary world, judgment is not seen as a hopeful action. Why would a world without judgment and justice be hopeless?

2. The good news of Christianity is not only that our sins are forgiven, but also that this world will know the same justice as heaven knows. Meditate on why this is good news.

3. The heart of the gospel is that God is both the just one and the justifier of those who trust Jesus. Why does this gospel actually establish divine justice?

6

In the Lion's Den: Learning to trust a God of power

"I am His wheat, ground fine by the lion's teeth to be made purest bread for Christ. Better still, [you should] incite the creatures to become a sepulcher for me; let them not leave the smallest scrap of my flesh, so that I need not be a burden to anyone after I fall asleep. When there is no trace of my body left for the world to see, then I shall truly be Jesus Christ's disciple." Those were Ignatius of Antioch's words as he wrote to the Romans in advance of his arrival there. All we know is that he received his wish: he died in the Flavian Amphitheater, sometime during the reign of the Roman Emperor Trajan (between A.D. 98 and 117). Ignatius was killed by lions.

In this, Ignatius was not terribly unusual. There were cycles of persecution and martyrdom in the early church, when emperors decided that it was to their advantage to enforce their understanding that the empire could only hold together if all worshiped Roman gods. And in those times of Roman persecution, hundreds at a time would die as they remained true to the affirmation that Jesus alone was Lord.

We often think that this type of persecution was the remnant of a by-gone age. What most of us fail to realize is that, historians tell us, there were more martyrs for the Christian faith in the twentieth century than in the previous nineteen centuries combined. And it appears that the present century may be even bloodier for those who profess faith in Christ. Whether in Islamic countries such as Sudan, Saudi Arabia, Iraq, or Afghanistan, in unstable countries such as Rwanda or Indonesia, or in Communist nations such as China, North Korea, or Laos, contemporary Christians face imprisonment and death for their faith in Jesus.

We look at our lives and they seem far away from Ignatius or the countless, nameless modern martyrs. I would suggest that there are parallels that are closer to home; though it may look different, the opposition and persecution we face for the gospel can cause a similar kind of pain and sorrow. When one's spouse doesn't understand the other's devotion to Jesus and tries to persuade her not to go to church; when one's boss threatens termination if he doesn't look the other way when an unethical deal goes down; when we are falsely accused, when we are opposed out of someone else's jealousy, when we suffer for doing right – in short, when we are opposed and persecuted for serving our God and for living lives of integrity, we know and taste a little of how it feels to witness in the way Ignatius and other saints did.

In those times of struggle and opposition, persecution and witness, we long for God to demonstrate his strength, his might, and his power. What we discover in Daniel 6 is that the praise of God which the pagan king Darius gives at the end of the chapter is true: our God "delivers and rescues; he works signs and wonders in heaven and on earth, he who has saved Daniel from the power of the lions'" (6:27). God is powerful, able to save his people from the forces, powers, and circumstances of their lives.

But what we will also discover is this: the power of God is not displayed ultimately in his ability to rescue and deliver; rather, the power of God is displayed in his ability to take evil and transform it for good and for his own purposes. And we believe this because our God is the one who raised the crucified Jesus from the dead, transforming the unimaginable evil of the crucifixion into the inconceivable glory of the resurrection.

The Lion's Den

One of the difficulties we have with this story is that it is so familiar. As a result, we struggle to hear it afresh. We know, for example, that God's promise through the prophet Jeremiah that Babylon would be utterly destroyed, never to be rebuilt, came true (Jer. 51:62). The Medes and Persians ruled jointly over a vast empire. We know that Darius set up an administration for the Persians that centralized power in three presidents, who reported to him; and chief among these presidents was the aged Daniel himself. We know that Daniel began to distinguish himself once again among his colleagues, so much so that Darius wanted to set him over the whole kingdom (6:3). We know as well that his colleagues in the administration didn't like this and decided to take Daniel down. They were motivated by jealousy, of course. And the only grounds they could find on which to accuse Daniel was his devotion to God; they took his strong point and tried to make it a liability.

And so, as we know, they set a trap for Daniel. These enemies enlisted the entire administration — "these presidents and satraps came by agreement" — to go to the king and convince him to pass a law "that whoever makes petition to any god or man for thirty days, except to you, O king, shall be cast into the den of lions" (6:6, 7). The king, flattered by their recognition of his godlike status, agreed. And here was the parallel to Daniel 3: in that chapter, all the government officials were to worship Nebuchadnezzar's "great feat" or be thrown into a fiery furnace; in this, all are to pray to Darius as a god or be thrown into a den of lions.

But notice verse 10: "When Daniel knew that the document had been signed ...." He was well aware of what was going on; it didn't come as a surprise to him. Likewise, it is striking that there didn't seem to be any debate in Daniel's mind about what he should do. There was no balancing or casuistry, no attempts to find a way around the king's degree, no indication of protest. He could have said to himself, "You know, I've been doing this prayer ministry a long time now. Perhaps I can cut it down to once a day while I'm falling asleep. Because, you know, I am getting up there; I'd like to make it to my ninetieth birthday." No, he didn't do that. He simply acted as he had: three times a day, with his window opened toward Jerusalem, he "prayed and gave thanks before his God, as he had done previously" (6:10).

Waiting for him were his colleagues, watching him from afar as he "made petition and plea before his God" (6:11). They immediately ran to the king, sniveling, with the same complaint that had been made against Daniel's friends in chapter 3: "Daniel, who is one of the exiles from Judah, pays no attention to you, O king" (6:13; cf. 3:12). These exiles from Judah, these outsiders who are so devoted to their God, these strangers who have strange ways, they pay no attention to you, king. They mock your authority; they are subversive and dangerous; they need to go.

The king was stricken because he liked Daniel and could see that he had been trapped. He tried to figure out a way to get Daniel out of this situation, but he couldn't because "it is a law of the Medes and Persians that no injunction or ordinance that the king establishes can be changed" (6:15).

And so, "the king commanded, and Daniel was brought and cast into the den of lions" (6:16). But the language here suggests that there was more than meets the eye – from the benediction the king gave to the first words the king said the next morning, we have the sense that both Daniel and his God were on trial: "May your God, whom you serve continually, deliver you!" (6:16). The stone was rolled over the den and the king went home for a sleepless night. At daybreak, the king went to the pit where Daniel was and cried out: "O Daniel ... has your God, whom you serve continually, been able to deliver you?" (6:20). That's the question: will God deliver Daniel? Was Daniel really innocent? Would they – Daniel and his God – be vindicated?

The answer was yes! Daniel shouted back, "My God sent his angel and shut the lions' mouths, and they have not harmed me, because I was found blameless before him; and also before you, O king, I have done no harm" (6:22). This was a miracle! It was not as though Daniel had brought steaks down with him and fed the lions in advance. And it was not as though Daniel brought a sleeping drug and administered it to the lions. How do we know? Not only because of what Daniel said, but also because of what happened to his accusers. The king brought them all – the men, their wives, and their children – and threw them in the pit: "And before they reached the bottom of the den, the lions overpowered them and broke all their bones in pieces" (6:24). In the same way that the fiery furnace had destroyed the seven men who had thrown Daniel's friends in it, so it was here. It was not as though the fire wasn't hot or the lions weren't hungry. No, this was a miracle: God demonstrated his power by rescuing Daniel. God was vindicated as a God of great power.

And that was why Darius sings. He actually issued a royal decree that mimicked the language we've noticed throughout Daniel's book: Daniel's God is the living God, the one who "delivers and rescues" by working "signs and wonders in heaven and earth." Even more, this God is the True King, "his kingdom shall never be destroyed and his dominion shall be to the end" (6:26-27). God's power was demonstrated, displayed, and vindicated in the rescue of Daniel.

The Lord's deliverance

Surely the Old Testament people of God understood the message here, especially in light of Daniel 3. There, Daniel's friends were cast into a fiery pit because they would not bow down and acknowledge Nebuchadnezzar as godlike. Here, in Daniel 6, Daniel was cast into a pit of lions because he would not bow down and pray to Darius as though he were godlike.

There, in Daniel 3, a fourth entered the fiery pit with the three friends, one like the Son of God; here, in Daniel 6, an angel, God's angel, the angel of the Lord, came and shut the mouths of the lions. There, the three friends emerged from the pit unharmed, even though it was hot enough to kill seven soldiers; here, Daniel emerged from the pit unharmed, even though the lions were hungry enough to devour the king's officials and their families before they hit the ground. There, the God of the three friends is exalted; here, the God of Daniel is praised.

Surely God's people should've gotten the message that their God is powerful to rescue and save. A God who could rescue from a fiery furnace and deliver from a lion's den was a powerful, mighty, sovereign God. There is none who can stay this God's hand, none who can question what he has done, none who can stop him or take him by surprise. Even though they were in a difficult place, where idolatry was rampant; even though they could believe that God had forgotten them; even though it may have appeared that

God was weak and unable to save because the Babylonians were victorious, God was clearly demonstrating to his people that he is Almighty God, powerful to save!

Sometimes that is hard to believe. We wonder whether God is paying attention to what is going on in our lives, whether he might be surprised by the pain and suffering that we are enduring, whether God was actually present when this evil happened. As we look back over our history, we wonder whether God wasn't able to rescue, wasn't strong enough to save. Or maybe it was the case that he didn't care, that he wanted to leave us alone, that he had, in fact, abandoned us.

But God's Word comes to us and reminds us: God is right there with us. He has not left us nor forsaken us. And he is able to deliver us from all our and his enemies. He is able to deliver us from the recent cancer diagnosis. He is powerful to preserve our lives or our children's lives in the situations we face. He is mighty to strengthen our hearts when a family member or co-worker who has no patience with the Christian gospel challenges our faith. He is powerful enough to deliver us from whatever lions may circle our lives.

But even more, our God is powerful and is able to turn tragedy, evil, and darkness to his own purposes, even when we can only wonder at what God has in mind. Such was the experience of Robert Bruce. He was one of the great Scots preachers in the generation after John Knox. Appointed to the pulpit of the Great Kirk of St Giles in Edinburgh when he was in his early thirties, his star rose rapidly. He became a favorite of King James; his sermons were published; and when he preached, thousands heard him. But then, when one of the king's allies murdered the Earl of Moray and was excommunicated from the church by a group led by Bruce, even though the king would not take legal action, he was furious with Bruce. Eventually, the king was able to secure Bruce's ouster from Edinburgh – for nearly thirty years, Bruce was unable to go to his home. Instead, he was exiled to the northernmost Scottish city, Inverness, a place that murdered Protestant preachers. He remained there seven years until he was allowed to return to the south, to the town of Larbert. But aside from six months during the reign of Charles I, he was unable to go home, and his influence was restricted to those who came to see him in these small towns.

On the surface, we cannot help but wonder why God allowed all this evil to befall Robert Bruce, a deeply pious minister of the gospel. But listen to what Bruce said toward the end of his life: "The Lord is a wonderful workman; he bringeth about his purpose that he can draw light out of darkness ... My enemies, the worst that they can do the Lord has turned into the best."

Catch that: *The worst that our enemies can do, the Lord can turn and has turned into the best*. Whatever it may be that we face, God is able to take the worst that our enemies can do and transform it into the best. Through our sorrow and pain, he draws us to himself and reveals his mercy in new ways. Through the opposition and persecution, he causes us to run to him in prayer and to cast ourselves in dependence upon him. Even in time, he brings us to develop a deep gratitude for them – some even come to the place of saying, "I would never have come to this level of love for Christ without or apart from this sorrow." God is working and displaying his power in our lives in order to transform the worst that our enemies can do into his best.

The Lord of Glory

But it is not only because of Daniel 6 that we know that God is a God of power who is able to transform the evil in our lives into good. We know this because we know Jesus. At the center of our faith is an understanding that this one who is the very Son of God and Savior of sinners; this one who went through life fulfilling the law of God, performing all righteousness from the moment of his birth to the moment of his death; this one who gave sight to those who were blind and unplugged ears that were deaf and raised men to life; this one who blessed children and welcomed sinners; this one who is absolutely innocent, pure, spotless, and holy – this one was crucified on trumped up charges in a horrible miscarriage of justice. When Jesus was nailed to the cross, it was an unspeakable act of evil – pure, unadulterated evil. It was a day of horrific evil, but it is the day that we call *Good* Friday.

And the reason we call it Good Friday is because on Easter Sunday God displayed his power in transforming unspeakable evil into unimaginable good through the resurrection of Jesus. One cannot help but see Christ's resurrection in this chapter. Like Daniel, Jesus was utterly innocent, blameless in the sight of all. Like Daniel, he was framed, trapped by jealous men who desired his destruction. In the same way that the Gentile authorities attempted to deliver Daniel, so Gentile authorities attempted to deliver Jesus. In the same way that Daniel was cast into the pit of death, so Jesus was buried in the pit of death. And, like Daniel, when the stone was rolled away, Jesus was alive. In his resurrection, his lifting out of the pit of death, the power of God was displayed. That's how evil Friday, black Friday, dark Friday, became Good Friday. It's because ultimately Resurrection Sunday came.

However, not only did the resurrection serve as the ultimate display of God's power in transforming evil into good. It also served to vindicate God and Jesus completely. In the same way that God and Daniel were vindicated when

God rescued Daniel from death, so God and Jesus were. Jesus had said that he was the Son of God and Savior of sinners; he had claimed that he and the Father were one; he had promised that those who came to the Father through him would be saved. But how to know whether Jesus was telling the truth?

With the crucifixion, it appeared that he was simply a deluded man or a master teacher, but not the Lord of glory. "We had hoped that he was the one to redeem Israel," but obviously he was not (Luke 24:21). Even more, it appeared that the devil himself had won; that the serpent had not simply bruised Jesus' heel, but had crushed him (cf. Gen. 3:15).

But then, the women returned with news: the Lord of Glory is alive! When the stone was rolled away, it was not moved in order to let Jesus out. It was moved as a testimony to the fact that Jesus was already raised from the dead. And by the very power of the resurrection, Jesus was vindicated before angels and demons, principalities and powers, men and women, boys and girls, from that day to this. He was who he said he was: the Son of God, Savior of sinners.

As we put our trust in Jesus, something remarkable happens. The same resurrection power that God used to raise Jesus from the dead is active in us. That's what Ephesians 1-2 tells us: the "immeasurable greatness of God's power toward us who believe" (1:19) was at work in our lives when God raised us from the spiritually dead, made us alive together with Christ, and seated us in the heavenly places in Christ. Indeed, the very fact that we love God and reverence him is proof that God is able to triumph over evil, sin, and injustice.

And so, in the darker places of our lives, when we doubt the power of God, we can look to Jesus. We can look to the powerful work God did in him, transforming the unspeakable evil of Good Friday into the unimaginable glory of

Easter Sunday. We look to the powerful work God does through him, transforming the unmentionable evil of our hearts into the undeniable, transforming progress of his glory. And we can believe that even if it is God's purpose that we suffer for a little while, we are "by God's power being guarded through faith for a salvation ready to be revealed in the last time" (1 Pet. 1:5). We can come to him and honestly admit that we sometimes wonder where he is; but we can also trust that he has been with us all along and is with us now. Even more, we can know this because we too are seated in God's own presence; we've been raised from the dead and know God's glory already. All this because we have come to believe and are united to the Lord of Glory who will, at the end of the age, display his great power and make all things new.

FOR FURTHER REFLECTION

1. All too often, as we know suffering, we long for rescue and deliverance. But a more amazing display of God's power is to bring good out of evil. How do Genesis 50:20 and Romans 8:28 relate to Daniel 6?

2. The parallels between Daniel 3 and Daniel 6 are important. Reflect again on them: why does the Holy Spirit emphasize these things through these two chapters? How should you respond?

3. The resurrection has served as a key foundation for our hopes in many of these chapters from Daniel. Why is that the case? Why does the picture of God in Daniel lead us to the resurrection of Jesus?

7
Kings and Kingdoms: Learning to trust a God who rules

It was three years later, and still the attack had deep repercussions in the citizens' hearts and minds. The people didn't really believe that their city, the eternal city, could fall to these strangers with strange ways, strange language, and strange looks. And yet it had happened. The strange invaders had triumphed over the most powerful army in the world and had ransacked their city for three days before withdrawing.

This defeat was more than a single defeat – it was a sign of the nation's downward turn, a sign of the end of an era. But now, three years later, people still wondered what had happened – where was God in all of this? How could he allow this apparently eternal city to know defeat? Others suggested that it was *because* people had trusted in the Christian God that this defeat came. The finger-pointing was dividing the city, but it was also bringing the Christian faith into disrepute, shaking the faith of some and emboldening others.

And so, a theologian-pastor, who lived a great distance from this mega-city, took up the task of explaining what

God was up to in the world – and not only the world in a cosmic, macro sense, but the world of these people who knew such a psychologically devastating defeat. He sat down at his desk and produced one of the classic theological expositions of all time. For to this day, Augustine's *City of God* continues to resonate as a way of understanding the relationship between the kingdoms of this world and the Kingdom of God.

In this book, Augustine describes two cities: the city of God, in which individuals adhere to Christ and have the possibility of leading virtuous lives; and the city of man, in which individuals place their trust in themselves and so live out of self-love. Christians live in this world as citizens of the city of God; while they may live in earthly cities such as Rome, Constantinople, or Carthage, or New York, London, Hong Kong, or Sydney, they live ultimately as those under God's rule, as those who belong to the city of God. The defeat of the earthly cities in which we live comes as the result of the city of man caving in on itself, undone by the selfish and untrammeled desire for power evidenced by unbelievers.

This way of thinking about the way Christians live in the world – the tension of belonging to two cities or two kingdoms – continues to have a great deal of weight and influence because it resonates both with the biblical material and our own experience. For example, we know biblical texts such as Philippians 3:20: "But our citizenship is in heaven, and from it we await a Savior, the Lord Jesus Christ." And we also know the tensions that come from being "sojourners and exiles" (1 Pet. 2:11) in this world. Because we do not belong to this world, those who live for the city of man hate and persecute believers (John 17:14-16). In the face of such tribulation and persecution, God calls us to live our lives in this place while maintaining our true loyalties to his kingdom and his rule.

Sometimes negotiating the tension between belonging to two cities or two kingdoms is difficult. Sometimes we become too comfortable here, too caught up in the political struggles of the kingdom of men, too fearful about what will happen if this person is elected or if this proposal passes. At other times, when we know opposition and persecution, when we know the crushing power of the kingdoms of men, we wonder where God is. We cry out at those times, "Lord, how long until you come to establish your reign perfectly, fully, and finally in the last days?"

How should we as believers negotiate this tension? Is there any hope for us as we live out this tension between the two kingdoms, the two cities?

The same question was undoubtedly asked by God's people as they lived out their time of exile, away from the Holy City, away from the now destroyed temple, away from the regular worship of their God. By the time this vision came to Daniel, it had been perhaps sixty years since Israel had been exiled to Babylon. Sixty years – in captivity, trying to negotiate the tension between living in Babylon and remaining loyal to Zion, between being citizens of Israel but also citizens of Babylon. They wondered, as those who lived under the rule of oppressive, pagan men, how it was possible to live as exiles in a foreign land and still be loyal to Yahweh, the King of kings and Lord of lords. Was there any hope for those who trusted in the God of Israel?

In the strange scenes of Daniel 7, we find great hope and comfort. For we find that while the kingdoms of men exercise their power in grotesque and oppressive ways – crushing their enemies with amazing strength and rapidity – there is a King who is ruling from on high. This King will bring these kingdoms to an end and will establish his own kingdom, which will last forever. This King will set up a courtroom and will judge all the nations of the earth. And this King is none other than our God, the Ancient of Days, who has come near to us in Jesus Christ our Lord.

The Kingdoms of men

One thing that strikes us immediately as the chapter opens is how strange the picture of these kingdoms was. "Four great beasts" came up out of a turbulent sea – and they were bizarre:

- There was a lion with eagle's wings, which were then plucked off in order to facilitate the lion's standing on two feet like a man (7:4).

- There was a bear, lying on its side, with three ribs between its teeth (7:5).

- There was a leopard with four heads and four wings of a bird on its back (7:6).

- There was a beast with iron teeth, claws of bronze, and ten horns – from these, a little horn that had human eyes and a loud mouth emerged. In front of this little, loud-mouthed horn, three other horns were plucked out by the roots (7:7-8).

As we read this, we can understand why the great sixteenth-century Reformer and Bible commentator, John Calvin, stopped his commentary on Daniel with chapter six! Immediately, we understand that this scene is different from the court narratives of the first part of the book and that it requires us to read the text differently. What we have here is the kind of literature that we know also from the book of Revelation. We sometimes call it "apocalyptic literature," but I tend to think of it as similar to science fiction in this sense: in the same way that science fiction uses bizarre, grotesque creatures to convey a single message, so here. These beasts are metaphors or pictures that represent the types of human kingdoms to come in Israel's future.

There seems to be a parallel between these beasts and the four types of metal in Nebuchadnezzar's statue in Daniel 2. And I think this was intentional – just as Daniel 4 and 5 go together and chapters 3 and 6, so Daniel 2 and 7 as well. The real question is who or what these beasts represent. The interpretation that carries the most weight sees these four beasts as representing four successive historical kingdoms: Babylon, Medo-Persia, Greece, and Rome.

While this approach has a great deal of merit, I tend to think that we might do as well to see these beasts as representing characteristics of the kingdom of men: the strength, power, and speed that can be brought to bear by these kingdoms in order to make their rule invincible. These beasts were grotesque and frightening, the kinds of things that we wouldn't want to meet in an alleyway. These beasts were able to devour, tear, and destroy. Even more, these kingdoms represented the terrifying rule of those who disobey the True King of the world. That was what made these beasts so frightening; they specifically targeted God's people. The kingdoms of man were pitted against believers in Yahweh: they exercised their power in ways that led to their harm; they "made war against the saints" (7:21); they persecuted and oppressed them, "wearing out the saints of the Most High" (7:25); and they exalted themselves by "speaking words against the Most High," defying God to intervene (7:25).

Now, we have to say that in Western countries, we don't know what this feels like, not to the same extent as our brothers and sisters in other parts of the world. What does this look like for them? In October 2005, the Voice of the Martyrs website detailed a horrific attack by a male Muslim on four Christian high school girls in Indonesia. While three of the girls were decapitated, a fourth girl survived the attack with a severe slash to her head and neck. She continues to heal physically and emotionally from this brutality. But because she lived in a Muslim-majority province, the government did nothing to bring her attacker to justice. There are countless stories like this as the kingdoms of men countenance or orchestrate persecution and oppression of the saints.

And yet, even in Western countries, we know a little of what it feels like to have someone exercise their power and rule in a brutal or oppressive fashion. It may be a university that refuses to allow a campus group to meet as an officially-recognized organization because it is a Christian organization that believes the Bible. It may be a workplace that fails to pay a living wage in a community that has systemic structures that maintain poverty. It may be a local community that has a homeowners' association that prevents someone from having a regular prayer meeting in their home. It may be a policy, ruling, or political amendment that perpetuates injustice to the weakest among us. And these governments and rulers sometimes exercise their authority with great speed and ferocity, forcing God's people to shudder and wonder when it will all stop.

Now, these matters aren't necessarily life or death, but they do make us long for things to be set to rights again. We wonder how long until the new song of God's justice will be sung. And so it is that when ruled by these kingdoms of men, from which there appears to be no deliverance, when worn out by the oppression of those who have power to harm us, when fearful of what may happen as we live in this place as strangers and exiles – our hearts need the comfort and hope that comes from the other part of this vision. We need to know that there is a True King that will exercise his rule over the whole earth one day.

The Kingdom of God

After these frightful visions of these horrific beasts, Daniel turned to see a courtroom scene that takes place on the earth: the Ancient of Days is seated upon his throne; a ridiculously large multitude serves him; and he sits in judgment upon these kingdoms. But where is the throne? The thrones are set in the midst of the world: "thrones were placed, and the Ancient of Days took his seat" (7:9). This tells us that God hasn't ceded this world over to the devil; this is God's world and he continues to rule over it. And where God's throne is, there is the place of judgment. He sets up his courtroom and opens the books in order to judge the kingdoms of men (7:10, 26).

Even more, though the kingdoms of men do their worst, they are stripped of their power and dominion. These kings who move with such speed and ferocity to execute their judgment against God's people are brought to nothing. Their authority is given to another, "one like a son of man" (7:13). To this one "was given dominion and glory and a kingdom, that all peoples, nations, and languages should serve him; his dominion is an everlasting dominion, which shall not pass away, and his kingdom one that shall not be destroyed" (7:14). Notice how this language parallels Daniel 4:34-35; the very dominion of God, the rule of God, will be granted to this one who was like a son of man.

Who was this one who was like a son of man? Daniel's scene doesn't give us an indication, other than to say that the Ancient of Days gives an everlasting kingdom to him. Surely, though, God's people would have recognized this one as the hoped-for Messiah. Surely, they would have heard strains of 2 Samuel 7 here, where God promised David, "I will raise up your offspring after you, who shall come from your body, and I will establish his kingdom. He shall build a house for my name, and I will establish the throne of his kingdom forever" (2 Sam. 7:12-13). Surely, they would have heard promises made through Isaiah, that a child would be born and that "of the increase of his government and of peace there will be no end, on the throne of David and over his kingdom, to establish it and to uphold it with justice and with righteousness from this time forth and forevermore" (Isa. 9:7).

Who was this one like a son of man? As Christians, we stand on this side of the cross and empty tomb and we hear echoes of Jesus. And that is because this title, "the Son of Man," was applied particularly to Jesus in Matthew's Gospel, chapter 16. There, in Caesarea Philippi, Jesus asked his disciples, "Who do people say that the Son of Man is?" After hearing their answers, he asked, "Who do you say I am?" Peter replied, "You are the Christ, the Son of the living God." In reply, Jesus affirmed Peter's answer and told all the disciples that the new community that he was building upon this confession would prevail against the gates of hell, the gates of these evil kingdoms empowered by the enemy himself (Matt. 16:13-18).

But how would Jesus, the Son of Man, the Christ, do this? How would Jesus establish his rule, reign, and realm? Not in the way that the disciples thought. Rather, "from that time Jesus began to show his disciples that he must go to Jerusalem and suffer many things from the elders and chief priests and scribes, and be killed, and on the third day be raised" (Matt. 16:21). The kingdom of God would come through redemptive suffering – the kingdoms of men, the kingdom of the devil and all his works, the kingdom of self, sin, and suffering all would come to an end because the King established his own kingdom by dying on a cross.

There would come a day when the crucified and resurrected Son of God, who was the Son of Man, would come to set the world to rights once again. In Matthew 16, Jesus promised that "the Son of Man is going to come with his angels in the glory of his Father" (Matt. 16:27). Here is a reference to Daniel 7:13: this cloud-riding Son of Man will come to set all things to rights, to receive dominion over the world and the obedience of the nations – but first, the glory of God's kingdom will be displayed through the cross and empty tomb.

This anchors our hope. Our hope and comfort as we live in the tension between the kingdoms of men and the kingdom of God are not simply that we will die and escape this place to live in an unpolluted heaven. No, our great hope is that one day Jesus will come on the clouds, we will rise, he will set this world to rights, and the kingdoms of this world shall be the kingdoms of our God and his Christ. Even more, this Christ will grant rule to his people: "the saints of the Most High shall receive the kingdom and possess the kingdom forever, forever and ever" (7:18). By virtue of our union with Jesus, as he rules, so will we. We will participate in his continuing rule and care of his world; the new heavens and new earth will be ours forever.

This means that the kingdom of God is not like the kingdoms of man. All too often, we get confused and merge the two. All too often, we are like that confused American Presbyterian from 1873 who stood on the floor of the General Assembly and said, "Nail the flag just below the cross, and stand by it, and if need be, die by it." Such a merging of our national flags with the cross represents a merging of the kingdoms of men with the kingdom of God. The cross is its own banner; it declares to a watching world that Jesus Christ alone is King. And even the king-doms of men in which we live and to which we are loyal will be judged one day.

There was another set of Presbyterians in history who were closer to the truth. In seventeenth-century Scotland, Presbyterians who refused to agree with their Anglican neighbors that the king was the head of the church came to be known as the Covenanters. Their rallying cries were "for Christ and his Kingdom" and "Christ's crown and covenant." One of the great Covenanters from this period was a man named James Guthrie. He had served as a pastor in the Church of Scotland and was one of the generation of Scots Presbyterians who welcomed the work of the West-minster Assembly. Upon the restoration of Charles II and the attempt to force Scots Presbyterians to bow the knee to Charles as the head of the church, Guthrie was forced from his pulpit, brought before the Privy Council, and condemned to die.

Guthrie was tried and condemned before the so-called 1661 "Drunken Parliament." Upon his condemnation, he gave a lengthy defense that concluded with these words: "My Lord, my conscience I cannot submit. But this crazy body and mortal flesh I do submit, to do with it whatso-ever you will, whether by death, or banishment, or impris-onment, or anything else; only I beseech you to ponder well what profit there is in my blood. It is not the extin-guishing of me or of many others that will extinguish the Covenant or work of the Reformation since the year 1638. My blood, bondage or banishment will contribute more for the propagation of these things than my life and liberty would do, though I should live many years."

On July 1, 1661, James Guthrie was hanged. His head was taken from his body and placed on a pike in Aberdeen, so that people might see what happens to those who disobey the kingdoms of man. And yet, James Guthrie was right. We know he was right because we still talk about James Guthrie today; and we talk even more about James Guthrie's God. This God who had saved Guthrie through his covenant of grace; this God whom Guthrie honored as the great King of the world; this God continues to rule over his people and to be worth dying for. We may someday have to be like James Guthrie, willing to offer our lives as a testimony that the kingdom of God is far to be preferred to the kingdoms of men. But the great hope is that our dying will not be wasted, because there is coming a day in which the court will sit in judgment, a day in which the powers of the kingdoms of men will be stripped away. And the wonder of God's grace is this: because of our union with Christ, our union with this Son of Man, and because he reigns, we will reign too.

For Further Reflection

1. Does Augustine's account of the two cities make sense of Daniel 7? How might it provide a way of negotiating the tensions we feel belonging to God's city and living in man's?

2. What are some ways that you have experienced the brutal or oppressive rule of the kingdoms of man for your faith in God? How does Daniel 7 offer you hope?

3. Because Jesus, the Son of Man, rules, we will too. How might this shift the way we view the less-than-ultimate political struggles of our own day?

8

Prophecy and History: Learning to trust a God who orders everything

Nowadays, the comics are not that funny. However, sometimes I still get a chuckle from the comics in the *New Yorker* magazine. One of my favorites depicted a man with shaggy hair, dressed in a robe, looking very dour and holding a sign. The sign said, "The End is Near." Next to this man was a woman also with shaggy hair, dressed in a robe, holding a sign. This woman was presumably his wife, because she was holding a sign that said, "You wish!"

Our modern prophets often prophesy of the end, and yet they disappoint us in all kinds of ways. One such "prophet" was William Miller, who concluded after studying his Bible that Jesus was going to return sometime between March 1843 and March 1844. And so, he gathered his followers and convinced them to sell all their possessions. They went on top of a mountain, wearing white robes, awaiting Jesus' return. When Jesus didn't return by March 1844, Miller went back and recalculated, saw an error, and set the new date: October 1844. When that month came and went, Miller gave up his calculations, but his followers continued to believe. And these believers became known as the Seventh Day Adventists after their two most prominent beliefs: that the seventh day of the week is the Sabbath and that Jesus would return in his second advent at any moment.

Miller wasn't the only prophet of his kind. Even in recent times, there have been those who have prophesied about the end of time: whether 1988 or 1994 or Y2K, various Bible teachers have prophesied doomsday. But each doomsday has come and each doomsday has passed, and many Christians have been left behind disappointed. Take all of this together with the incredible phenomenon of the "Left Behind" novels, with over 60 million copies sold, and the various television preachers who attract huge followings for their "prophetic insight" – it is understandable why some have become cynical about whether the Bible can really tell us anything about the future. After all, history is littered with people who have tried to understand the prophecies of the Bible and who have failed.

And so, the question confronts us: does the Bible really tell us about the future? Can we be sure about anything the Bible says when it comes to prophecy? While it is understandable that we would be cynical or skeptical about these things, such attitudes would be a mistake. And that is because the Christian faith rests on the ability of our God to say things about the future and for them to come true. The prophet Isaiah taught this in Isaiah 46:8-10:

> *Remember this and stand firm, recall it to mind, you transgressors, remember the former things of old; for I am God, and there is no other; I am God, and there is none like me, declaring the end from the beginning and from ancient times things not yet done, saying, "My counsel shall stand, and I will accomplish all my purpose."*

What did God say here? He said that his very credibility as God rests on the fact that he declares the end from the beginning and things not yet done from ancient times. Even more, God's credibility as God rests on the fact that he purposes things and that they happen exactly as he purposes. It is not as though God looks down the corridor of time, sees what is going to happen through human agency, and then declares things to be so. No, what Isaiah 46 clearly claims is that God decrees, and that's why things happen; God purposes, and that's why he knows. Our God is a God who has the power and ability to order all things.

All this is particularly important for understanding Daniel 8. To this point, God has repeatedly declared and demonstrated that he is the True King of the world, that he is the one ruling over history, and that his purposes for Babylon, Israel, and the church will be accomplished. And yet, as we've seen, some of these prophecies are difficult to understand even as we look backwards through history. After all, they've dealt with various metals in a strange statue destroyed by a large boulder and horrifying beasts with speaking horns that are trumped by the Ancient of Days who sets his throne on the earth. God doesn't provide the "answer key" to these prophecies, and so it is difficult to identify exactly what he meant.

But here in Daniel 8, God gives both prophecy and interpretation. And in doing so, he provides great encouragement for his people, because he demonstrates that he is the Lord of history and the King of time, the one who orders all things to bring great glory to himself.

For God's people, languishing in exile in Babylon, such words of prophecy and history would have encouraged. After all, by the time of this prophecy, it was approximately 550 B.C.; God's people had been in captivity for nearly forty years. The questions might have circled around in their hearts and minds: why did God allow the evil Babylonians to triumph over them? How long would their suffering continue – had God utterly abandoned them? And what about God's promises about a Redeemer who would come to rule over God's people forever? What about the promises of Daniel 7 about one like a son of man who would receive "an everlasting dominion, which shall not pass away" (7:14)? When would he come?

These questions echo with us: as a people that often feels in exile from our true home with God, we struggle with doubts about God's goodness and power. We look at our world and we wonder why God allows evil apparently to triumph. Why does God allow his servants to die for his testimony? Has God abandoned his people? Even more personally, we look at our hearts and lives, our struggles with sin, addictions, doubts, and fears, and we cry out with the Apostle Paul, "Wretched man that I am! Who will deliver me from this body of death?" (Rom. 7:24).

Texts such as Daniel 8 should encourage our hearts and give us hope. This close connection between prophecy and history teaches us that God is the ruler who is able to order all things to accomplish his will: he is the Lord of history and King of time. He ordered the rise and fall of Media and Persia, Greece and Rome; he ordered the coming of Jesus Christ "when the fullness of time had come" (Gal. 4:4); he has ordered everything for Christ's return; and he has ordered the individual moments of our lives so that even as evil happens to us, God orders it for our salvation.

Words of prophecy
Many Bible scholars see this chapter as a key for the visions that have gone before – unlike Daniel 2 and the huge statue of multiple metals, and unlike Daniel 7 with four strange beasts, here the animals were identified. As

a result, many interpreters relate these two beasts to the others that have gone before. And Daniel himself seemed to suggest that we should do so: "In the third year of the reign of King Belshazzar a vision appeared to me, Daniel, after that which appeared to me at the first" (8:1). This connects Daniel 7 and 8, as though Daniel were saying, "After I had the strange and mysterious dream of Daniel 7, two years later I had a dream that seemed connected to the first one."

Of course, taken on its face, Daniel 8 is equally strange and mysterious. Daniel saw himself in Susa, which was a fortified city in the province of Elam and would become a favorite place for the Medo-Persian rulers (see Esther and Nehemiah). He was transported to the side of a canal. While he was there, he saw a ram with two horns, both of which were tall but one of which was a bit higher than the other. This ram ran north, west, and south, conquering everything before him.

But, then, a male goat came from the west, running so fast that he was not even touching the ground. The goat had one large horn, and he used it to strike the ram, break its two horns, and cast him to the ground. The goat became incredibly great until, at the height of his strength, his horn was broken. Out of this single horn came four smaller horns. One of these horns became strong, particularly in the south and toward "the glorious land" (9). That horn became great, challenging the "Prince of the host," transgressing "the regular burnt offering" for a short space of time (8:11-12). After a length of time (2,300 days), somehow the sanctuary would be restored to its proper use.

The vision-dream was exceedingly strange – and Daniel desperately desired to know its interpretation. In the same way that we sometimes will wander into the kitchen after having a bizarre dream to tell our spouses, so Daniel "sought to understand it" (8:15). And God in his mercy shouted, "Gabriel, make this man understand the vision!" (8:16). This angelic personage, Gabriel, came to Daniel – this was the first of several visits by Gabriel, both in this book and later in biblical history (see Luke 1:8-23, 26-38). Gabriel told him the interpretation of the vision-dream. What shocks us as we read Gabriel's interpretation is this: what he told Daniel as future prophecy, we read as past history.

Witness of history
Twice, Gabriel noted that what Daniel saw was about "the end": "Understand, O son of man, that the vision is for the time of the end" (8:17); "I will make known to you what shall be at the latter end of the indignation, for it refers to the appointed time of the end" (8:19). How should we understand "the end" here? Gabriel was not talking about the final end, the end of history and time when God brings about the new heavens and the new earth. Rather, he was talking about the end of this era of exile and God's apparent absence.

For hundreds of years, God's people knew his voice, his presence, his comfort; but there would come a time, after their return to the Promised Land, when God's people would know his silence. That time, which we call "the inter-testamental period," was a period in which a great deal happened: nations would vie for Palestine like football players chasing a fumble; Israel would work to maintain its sense of identity in a rapidly, regularly changing world; and the temple would still be the focus of Israel's hopes even as the synagogue system would develop. What Gabriel said in this prophecy had to do with the end of exile and this period of silence. And if God's people would pay attention, they would know exactly what was going to happen – because God is the Lord of history and the King of time, the one who orders all things because he rules over all things.

And so, Gabriel told Daniel that the ram represented the kings of Media and Persia (8:20). These two kingdoms would dominate the Middle East for over two hundred years, from around 550 B.C. to 330 B.C.; their rule would extend from modern-day India west through Turkey into Greece and south through Babylon to Palestine, Egypt, and sections of modern-day Libya. Just as the ram went "westward and northward and southward" (8:4), so the Medo-Persia Empire went west, north, and south. But this empire was an unstable alliance: just as one horn was bigger than the other in the vision (8:3), so one part of the empire, the Persian part (which equates to modern-day Iran), was stronger than the other and would come to dominate in the end. It was Persia that would produce mighty warriors: Cyrus, Xerxes I, Darius the Great. They would rule the known world as well as the "glorious land."

Eventually, the Medo-Persian empire was challenged by a power from the west (8:5): Gabriel tells us that this power, typified by the goat, was Greece (8:21). After Philip of Macedon died in 336 B.C., his son Alexander succeeded him. And this Macedonian king would consolidate his power in Greece and in the space of thirteen years would conquer the known world. He dominated the known world so quickly that it appeared as though he was flying, not even "touching the ground" (8:5). The first major battle between Greece and Persia occurred in 333 B.C. at Issus, where Darius III fled the battle scene in such haste that he left his wife, daughters, and personal belongings. The second and finally decisive battle occurred at Gaugamela in 331 B.C., a fight so creative in battle tactics on Alexander's side that military historians continue to study them.

But Alexander's power was short-lived; he died in 323 B.C. at the age of thirty-three. By 301 B.C., his empire was divided into four districts, ruled by four families ("four conspicuous horns" [8:8, 22]): Macedonia; Thrace and modern-day Turkey; Babylon, Persia, and Palestine; and Egypt. These four districts "shall arise from his nation, but not with his power" (8:22). And that was what happened: none of these districts had the power that Alexander had; none were able to consolidate these four districts into a single empire, though that didn't stop some leaders from trying.

The empire that ruled most of the Middle East, including Palestine, was called the Seleucid Empire, which ruled this area from 312 to 64 B.C. This was the "horn" that had grown "exceedingly great toward the south, toward the east, and toward the glorious land" of Palestine (8:9). The Seleucids were the most powerful of the various districts and would be the final one to fall to the Romans when they were able to consolidate and extend Alexander's old empire.

Toward the end of Seleucid rule, according to Gabriel, a "king of bold face" would arise (8:23). "His power shall be great ... he shall cause fearful destruction and shall succeed in what he does, and destroy mighty men and the people who are the saints" (8:24). This king was most likely Antiochus IV Epiphanes, literally "the Shining One," who ruled the Seleucids from 175 to 163 B.C. He had a reputation for wisdom because he delighted in and promoted Greek philosophy and culture; he was a "Hellenist" who sought the riddles and wisdom of the east for his people (23). Antiochus waged a nearly successful war against the Egyptians, but was forced to withdraw. In revenge, he laid siege against Jerusalem around 168 B.C., which led to the massacre of a number of Jews and to the destruction of the city. Most notably, Antiochus ordered the cessation of the sacrifices in the rebuilt temple in 167 B.C. and profaned the temple by introducing a holy object sacred to the god Zeus to which he sacrificed a pig. In doing this, Antiochus took a stand against "the Prince of princes," God himself, by profaning the temple and the worship of the true and living God. And God himself would hold him accountable by taking his life: for Antiochus died in 164 B.C. as the result of a mysterious internal disease. He was "broken – but by no human hand" (8:25), just as God had said.

Promises of hope

Now, why is this lengthy history lesson important? It is important because God through Gabriel told Daniel all these things around 550 B.C.; these are events that played out over the next four hundred years or so exactly as he said. It is important because our God, who spoke worlds into existence, also spoke about these things long before they happened, and they happened just as he said. And that is important because this connection between prophecy and history gives us great hope. We have hope because God is the Lord of history and the King of time. Because he is the Alpha and Omega, we can trust this: what he says he will do, he does.

And while that is important when it comes to Darius, Cyrus, Alexander, and Antiochus, this relationship between prophecy and history is especially important when it comes to Jesus. Because all throughout the Bible, God said that he would send a Redeemer, a Messiah, a Savior. Promises were made at the earliest days; prophets were sent to speak in advance about this happening. And it all happened just as God said.

Think back through the Old Testament to the very beginning of the Bible. In Genesis 3:15, God told the serpent, his great enemy, that God would give the woman an offspring who would crush the serpent's head. From the very beginning of the biblical story, God's people were taught to expect an offspring of Eve who would destroy the enemy of our souls and who would set the world to rights again.

God comes to Abraham in Genesis 12 and promises him an offspring and a land; he also promises that through Abraham and his offspring, the families of the earth would be blessed. And through the child of promise, Isaac, and the ultimate child of promise, Jesus, that would be the case. In Genesis, God continues to promise that a King would come; through Jacob, he declares that it was through Judah, the fourth-born but most noble, that a ruler would come who would receive the scepter and the tribute (Gen. 49:10).

And the prophecies continue: there would be a prophet like Moses, who would declare God's Word and will perfectly (Deut. 18:15); he would be a priest like Aaron and yet one with an eternal lineage (Ps. 110:4); he would be a king like David, but one that would rule forever (2 Sam. 7:13). Isaiah predicted that this coming Davidic king would be the virgin-born Immanuel, God with us (Isa. 7:14); he would be a child who would bear government upon his shoulders (Isa. 9:6); he would be the righteous branch springing from David's stump (Isa. 11:1); he would be the servant who did all that Israel failed to do (Isa. 42:1-9); and he would be the servant who would suffer so that God's wayward, sinful people might be forgiven and healed (Isa. 53:4-6). Micah told us that the promised redeemer would be born in Bethlehem (Micah 5:2); Zechariah claimed that he would be a King riding upon the foal of a donkey (Zech. 9:9); Malachi, the last voice of God for 420 years or so, promised that one like Elijah would come to prepare the way (Mal. 4:5).

Is the point clear? Our faith rests on the fact that God said what he was going to do, and he did it all in Jesus Christ. And that is why Daniel 8 is so important. God is the Lord of history and the King of time; he is able to order all things to accomplish his purposes in our world and in our lives. He says what he is going to do, and he is able to do it.

Now, what does that mean for us? It means that we not only have a Savior in whom we can trust, who is faithful, a Savior who is the promised prophet, priest, king. It also means that in our lives, there is nothing that occurs outside the purposes of God. There are no free molecules in the universe, as theologian R. C. Sproul reminds us. There's nothing that happens by accident, by fortune, or by luck. Even more, far from randomness, our God orders everything in such a way that the plan he has for us is far superior to any we could possibly make for ourselves. As hard as it may be sometimes, as much pain as it causes, because God is the Lord of history and the King of time and because he orders all things in such a way that he receives glory and we know salvation, we can trust him.

The Heidelberg Catechism, that great doctrinal standard of the sixteenth century, reminds us of this truth. In the midst of the glorious first answer to the question, "What is your only comfort in life and in death?" the catechism tells us, "[Jesus] also watches over me in such a way that not a hair can fall from my head without the will of my Father in heaven: in fact, all things must work together for salvation." How is it possible to believe that? It is only possible when we realize that our God is the Lord of history and the King of time, that he has ordered all things for his glory and our good, and that the struggles and afflictions, the suffering and sorrow, of our lives are purposed by God to work for our salvation. And that gives us hope.

FOR FURTHER REFLECTION

1. While many believers study prophecy to understand the future, Daniel 8 grows our faith because it refers to things now past. What lessons should we take from this as we study prophecy?

2. Our faith is built upon the fact that God accomplishes all that he says he will do. Why is that important as a buttress for our faith in Jesus?

3. What are places in your life where the confidence that God is the Lord of history and the King of time is a firm rock of hope?

9

Confession, Mercy, Hope: Learning to trust a God of forgiveness

One of the remarkable features of the American Civil War was the number of fast days proclaimed by each side. American President Abraham Lincoln proclaimed three national fast days; the Confederate president Jefferson Davis prescribed nine, many of these as the war turned sour. The idea for these national fast days, north and south, was that the respective nations would mourn their national sins, repent, and ask God for mercy and to honor their war efforts. Not everyone was happy with these days of national mourning and repentance. General Ulysses S. Grant, for example, complained, "I would not have the anniversaries of our victories celebrated, nor those of our defeats made fast days and spent in humiliation and prayer."

And even Lincoln himself, toward the end of the war, would wonder about the propriety of the two sides of the one American nation competing before God's throne. In his Second Inaugural, he noted,

> *Both read the same Bible and pray to the same God, and each invokes His aid against the other. It may seem strange that any*

men should dare to ask a just God's assistance in wringing their bread from the sweat of other men's faces, but let us judge not, that we be not judged. The prayers of both could not be answered. That of neither has been answered fully. The Almighty has His own purposes.

While fast days didn't make much sense to men like Grant and Lincoln, to previous generations of Americans, such national fast days made plenty of sense. Part of the reason that these fast days made sense to many Americans was that they believed, wrongly, that God had a national covenant with America. Rooted especially in the way New England Puritans read the Old Testament and related God's covenant with Israel to their own colonies, Americans have believed that theirs was a "Redeemer Nation" that was called to spread freedom and democracy to the rest of the world. What this way of thinking fails to recognize, in my estimation, is that the lines of continuity run not between Israel and America, but between Israel and the church. After all, God's promise to Israel that they would be a "holy nation" (Deut. 7:6) and "a people for his own possession" (Exod. 19:5) were applied to the church by the Apostle Peter in 1 Peter 2:9. It is the people of God, centered on the Messiah Jesus, who have God's covenant promises and who form God's covenant nation.

In addition, this equation of Israel and America fails to see the uniqueness of God's relationship with his Old Testament people. That special, covenantal relationship between God and his people drove the profound questions that Israel had as they continued to suffer in exile from the Promised Land. After all, God had promised to be Israel's God and for them to be his people. He had promised to keep Israel as his "treasured possession among all peoples." He had promised that Israel would be "a kingdom of priests and a holy nation." And he had promised that David's sons would establish his kingdom and rule forever (Exod. 19:6; 2 Sam. 7:13).

But now, they were in exile, resident aliens among the wicked Babylonians. Even more, they had been in captivity for over sixty years – this vision had come "in the first year of Darius," at the beginning of Persian rule, 539 B.C. (9:1-2). Things were going from bad to worse – this people which had been conquered and exiled by the Babylonians were now being ruled by the Medes and the Persians. And they had to be wondering: God, how long? How are you going to keep your promises? How are you going to display to the nations that we are still your treasured possession? Have you dropped your side of the bargain? How are you going to deliver us? *Will* God deliver us? Is there any hope?

As God's people raised these questions, they should have heard the message of this chapter as the central point of Daniel's entire book. It is not too much to claim that all that Daniel has said was leading to this scene. Through the stories of the exemplary figure Daniel and through the strange imagery of Daniel's visions, God was telling his people that he had not forgotten them, that he had not abandoned them; God was telling his people that he was faithful, strong, able to save, the Lord of history and the True King of the world. Throughout these words and this Word, God called out to his people to forsake their false idols and false hopes, to turn from the broken cisterns that could hold no water, and to turn to him, the true, living, satisfying God (Jer. 2:13).

Confronted by the reality of their exile, the exposure of their idols as false, and the glories of the true and living God, God's people should have responded in the same way that Daniel did – by confessing their sins, especially their sins of idolatry, and by begging God for forgiveness and mercy. Indeed, the great hope of Daniel 9 is that when God's people cry out to him in repentant faith with words of confession, God comes near with words of mercy and hope. In fact, as we will see, his assurance of pardon and forgiveness was already on the way, already being delivered. God was ready to forgive and restore his people once again.

But this lesson is not simply for Daniel's time; it is for ours as well. For it may well be that God has been leading us as Christians and churches through a time of suffering, opposition, persecution, loneliness, depression, maybe even despair. God may have us in a place where we feel that we are in a pit, in exile, far from God. And God is calling out to us through our suffering and pain so that we might turn from our idols to trust the true and living God. It may be that God's Word in Daniel 9 for us is that we must repent and confess so that we might know our God once again as a God of forgiveness and mercy. Because when we confess our sins, he is faithful and just to forgive, cleanse, and restore (1 John 1:9).

Confession

In a way similar to the first six chapters of this book, Daniel serves as an exemplary character here as well. The focus, of course, is not on Daniel as a hero; rather, the focus is on Daniel's example of turning to his heroic God. For in offering these words of confession for his and his people's sins, he served as an example of what all of God's people, living as resident aliens, ought to do.

As we consider the context of Daniel's prayer of confession, we see that Daniel was motivated to confess his and his people's sins to God through his *reading of God's Word*. In verse 2, Daniel noted that "I, Daniel, perceived in the books the number of years that, according to the word of the Lord to Jeremiah the prophet, must pass before the end of the desolations of Jerusalem, namely, seventy years."

Daniel was referring to Jeremiah 25:8-12 and 29:10. In those places, God had declared:

> *Because you have not obeyed my words, behold, I will send for all the tribes of the north, declares the Lord, and for Nebuchadnezzar ... my servant ... This whole land shall become a ruin and a waste, and these nations shall serve the king of Babylon seventy years. Then after seventy years are completed, I will punish the king of Babylon and that nation, the land of the Chaldeans, for their iniquity, declares the LORD (Jer. 25:8-9, 11-12).*

The book of Jeremiah also says, "For thus says the LORD: when seventy years are completed for Babylon, I will visit you, and I will fulfill to you my promise and bring you back to this place" (Jer. 29:10).

This reading of God's Word had convinced Daniel of two things. First, he was convinced that the exile was the result of the sins of God's people; God had taken them into exile to punish their sin of idolatry. But second, God's Word convinced Daniel that there would be a time when God's indignation toward his people would be complete. There would be an end to the judgment and wrath of God; there would be a time of deliverance and hope. God himself had promised in Jeremiah 29 that he would visit them, that he would draw near, that he would bring them back to the holy land.

Equally important, Daniel *remembered God's covenant*. This covenantal structure supported Daniel's entire prayer. Throughout the Pentateuch, God had repeatedly told Israel that if they obeyed him, they would know blessing; but if they disobeyed him, they would know cursing and exile. For example, in Deuteronomy 28, God had warned his people that if they were "not careful to do all the words of this law that are written in this book," then "the LORD will scatter you among all peoples, from one end of the earth to the other, and there you shall serve other gods of wood and stone, which neither you nor your fathers have known" (58, 64).

One of the things, therefore, that drove Daniel's prayer was his recognition that his people, God's people, had disobeyed God, broken God's covenant, and violated faithfulness toward him and his Word. Israel went into exile believing that God had been unfaithful to them, that God had not kept his side of the covenant, that God had abandoned them. What Daniel discovered was that the issue wasn't that God had been unfaithful to Israel; rather, the problem was that Israel had been unfaithful to God.

And so, Daniel stood before God as Israel's representative, freely admitting and repeatedly stressing that though God had proven faithful to his people, God's people had sinned against him:

- "We have sinned and done wrong and acted wickedly and rebelled, turning aside from your commandments" (5).

- "To us, [belongs] open shame ... because of the treachery that they have committed against you" (7).

- "All Israel has transgressed your law and turned aside, refusing to obey your voice" (11).

Daniel recognized and confessed that God's people had sinned. He agreed with God that they were in the wrong and that God was in the right. But he went further: he also confessed that God's anger and discipline had come against them for their sins: "And the curse and oath that are written in the Law of Moses the servant of God have been poured out upon us, because we have sinned against him" (9:11b).

And yet, God's people until now had remained unrepentant: "Yet we have not entreated the favor of the LORD our God, turning from our iniquities and gaining insight by your truth" (9:13). How amazing was this! For sixty years, God's people had been in exile; for sixty years, they had questioned God's justice; for sixty years, they had wondered whether God was still present with them. Never once did they connect the dots and see that the exile was the result of their sin; their suffering was the result of their rebellion.

Though exile and judgment were thoroughly deserved and though they had remained unrepentant to this point, Daniel begged God's forgiveness and mercy on behalf of all God's people. And he began his confession by grounding his plea in two things: the honor of God's name and the greatness of God's mercy.

Especially in verses 17-19, Daniel argued first that the longer that God's people were in exile, the more dishonor would come to God's name. After all, Jerusalem and Israel had become a "byword among all who are around us" (9:16); the city, the one "that is called by your name," was desolate (9:18); and God must act to save his city and his people who were "called by your name" (9:19). God's own reputation as a God of justice and mercy, holiness and compassion, steadfast love and forgiveness would be drawn into question; his name was at stake.

Even more, second, God's mercy needed to be displayed. Daniel begs that God would "listen to the prayer of your servant and to his pleas for mercy" (9:17). God should listen not because of Daniel's or the people's righteousness, but "because of your great mercy" (9:18). God's very character as a God of mercy and a God of honor was on trial.

And so, Daniel's confession serves as a pattern for our own confessions of sin to our God, both corporately and individually. We should agree with God that we have sinned; that we have violated God's covenant and wandered away from God's Word; and that we have remained stiff-necked and unrepentant to this point. But we should also plead with God for forgiveness and mercy, pointing to his character as a God of mercy and his reputation as a God of honor, pointing to our covenantal relationship with him. Would not God forgive us for the fame of his name?

As we look around at evangelical churches, we recognize, in many parts of the world, our unfaithfulness and our idolatry of personalities, power, and prominence. We have preached a gospel of success and prosperity, whether material or intellectual, and have failed to honor God as the God of judgment and salvation. Some of our most prominent leaders and spokesmen have fallen into sexual sin and yet have remained undeterred from seeking the limelight. And I can't help but wonder if our reaction to our sins has simply been to wag our heads and wonder, rather than to engage in a season of confession, pleading for God's mercy in response to our self-sufficiency and our failure to depend fully on the only one who can save and transform us and advance his Kingdom.

In a similar way, we as individuals may be going through a difficult season – a time of opposition, persecution, anxiety. Perhaps God has brought a difficult season into our lives to get our attention, to shake us awake to the reality of our empty pursuit of the idols of our hearts. Perhaps it has been a while since we have sought God's face and turned our hearts to him. Perhaps we have been like God's people of old, failing to name our sins before God and others, failing to entreat the favor of the Lord.

God's Word is calling us to a time of introspection and examination in the light of God's Word – are there ways in which God is using the events of our lives to get our attention, to show us places where we have been unfaithful to him? If so, then run to him; make a sincere and genuine confession of your sins. Plead not righteousness, not good deeds, but plead the mercy of God.

Indeed, the good news for us Christians is that the mercy and honor of God has a name: Jesus. In him, justice and mercy meet; his obedience and satisfaction, his death and resurrection, ground God's mercy and vindicate God's honor. In him, God is both just and the justifier, both honored and merciful. And that's why we sing:

> Thy works, not mine, O Christ, speak gladness to this heart;
> They tell me all is done; they bid my fear depart.
>
> Thy pains, not mine, O Christ, upon the shameful tree,
> Have paid the law's full price and purchased peace for me.

We have a promise of mercy in Jesus – let us run to God and confess our sins pleading the blood and righteousness of our Savior.

Mercy and hope

Indeed, the great promise of Daniel 9 is that there is already a word of mercy on the way that meets us in our confession of sin. Notice, this word of mercy came "while I was speaking and praying." Twice, both in verse 20 and 21, Daniel noted this. As we draw near to God, as we confess our sins, what we find is that God is already there, ready with a word of pardon, mercy, and hope.

God had sent Gabriel, who came to Daniel again as he had in the previous chapter. He spoke these wonderful words: "At the beginning of your pleas for mercy a word went out, and I have come to tell it to you, for you are greatly loved" (9:23). God's love for us brings us into situations where we recognize our own failures; his steadfast love for us brings his Word to us and draws us to confess; and his great love brings to us a word of mercy in response to our plea.

And this word of mercy really is a word of hope. In Daniel's case, the word of hope was nothing less than an explanation of what God would do in the future. This, of course, brings us to the enigmatic prophecies of seventy weeks in Daniel 9:24-27. This explanation of Daniel's prophecy of seventy weeks continues to befuddle commentators and interpreters; one commentary I consulted listed nine possible scenarios for understanding how these seventy weeks-years relate to history.

Needless to say, I'm not going to take a stance on that. But I do believe that there is enough here to give God's people hope even if they do not understand fully the meaning of the prophecy of the seventy weeks. There are three things in particular to note: first, *there was a word going out to restore and rebuild Jerusalem* (9:25). To Daniel, this must have brought hope; he had just noted that Jerusalem was desolate and "under the whole heaven there has not been done anything like what has been done against Jerusalem" (9:12). But here was a word from God that Jerusalem would be rebuilt and restored; the temple, the symbol of God's presence with his people, would be reconstructed as well. And this would have given Daniel and his people hope: the time of absence and exile would come to an end.

Second, *there would be difficult times coming*. This word of warning pointed forward to a coming prince who would "destroy the city and the sanctuary." But even with the note of difficulty, there was hope: this wicked prince would not triumph ultimately, but would be judged finally: there was a "decreed end" to be "poured out on the desolator" (9:27).

Evil would not persist; evil men would be judged; all things would be set to rights at the end.

But third, *God is still in charge.* The words at the end of Daniel 9 remind us that nothing happens in our day that stands outside God's knowledge and control. Three times in the ESV the word "decreed" is used (9:24, 26, 27); if something is decreed, there must be someone decreeing it. If we have learned anything thus far from Daniel, it is that God is the True King of the world, the Lord of history and time. Though men might do their worst, nothing takes God by surprise. Nothing surprises him because he decreed it all, governing all his creatures and all their actions.

And that should give us hope. There is great hope in knowing that our God is in control. When our worlds are crashing around us and we are afraid, we must know that nothing happens to us without our Father's care and outside our Father's plan. And it very well may be that these times in our lives are meant to draw us nearer to God — through the confession of our sins and the breaking of our hearts.

Rose Marie Miller, in her book *From Fear to Freedom*, gave an account of how this happened in her life. As a pastor's wife, she always felt a bit better than others, a bit more righteous than the people to whom she and her husband Jack ministered. They had taken in homeless and unloved people and had shared the gospel in word and deed; and yet, she confessed that her self-righteousness had made her heart hard.

One time, Rose Marie and Jack had gone on a ski trip to the Alps. In the midst of a difficult time skiing, she wrestled with why God allowed her to go up a difficult mountain when she couldn't make it down. The answer came that Sunday: as her husband preached and then administered the Lord's Supper, she saw her hard heart. "As the loaf of

French bread was broken," she wrote, "it gave a crack. I saw with new eyes the spear of the soldiers breaking the body of Christ for my sins. My own heart broke as I remembered the ski incident of a few days before. It was as if God were saying to me, 'Rose Marie, your whole life is like your slide down that mountain. You are full of presumption, self-righteousness, and pride. I let you go up there to show you about yourself.'"

It very well may be that things have entered our lives in order for God to show us about ourselves: our hardened hearts, our idolatry, our lack of repentance. God, in his mercy, has let us slide down the mountain of life and broken our hearts in order to help us see ourselves as we are and himself as he is. Will you turn to the God who has come near in Jesus? Will you confess your sin? Will you let your heart be broken so that the fresh mercy of Jesus might be poured in, and so that you might have hope?

FOR FURTHER REFLECTION

1. As you look over the past several months, has God brought things into your life to highlight your need to repent and confess your sin to him? Will you make a determination to turn to him and plead his mercy?

2. Sometimes people "over-interpret" their circumstances and read everything as divine judgment. How might Daniel 9 encourage you to take your heart to the Lord for a time of discernment?

3. In what ways might confession serve to increase your hope?

10
The Real Battle:
Learning to trust God as
our faithful warrior

1992 was a consequential year in American politics. The incumbent Republican president, George H. W. Bush, ran against the Democratic nominee Bill Clinton and a late-entering independent named H. Ross Perot. And yet, none of those men gave the speech that was remembered from that campaign. The most important and remembered speech from the 1992 presidential election cycle was given by the defeated contender for the Republican nomination, the journalist Pat Buchanan.

Buchanan's speech on the Monday night of the Republican convention cast the Presidential election in apocalyptic categories. The most significant lines of the speech were:

My friends, this election is about much more than who gets what, it's about who we are. It's about what we believe. It's about what we stand for as Americans. There is a religious war going on in our country for the soul of America. It is a cultural war, as critical to the kind of nation we will one day become as was the Cold War itself.

These lines about a "culture war" actually were drawn from a then-recent academic book written by a sociologist at the University of Virginia. Buchanan drew from the academic discussion about the divides in American culture and inserted them into popular culture's conversation. And the language of "culture war" seemed to fit what people felt the situation was in America circa 1992.

Since that night, though, I've wondered whether Christians have become so caught up in the idea of a culture war that we've lost sight of the real battle. Because the real battle is not between Republicans and Democrats, or the secular left and the religious right; the real battle is among forces that are far greater, far more destructive, and, if you will, far more real.

We see evidence of the battle all around us. We see it in the fall of big steeple pastors – not just in sexual scandal, but in depression, discouragement, and despair. We see it in the break-up of marriages and the destruction of families. We see it in the drug and alcohol abuse and in the sexual addiction that chain so many. We see it in the anorexia and bulimia that have become an epidemic among our young women. We see it in the injustice and oppression that deny life to those within our cities. And though no one would suggest that many of these human actors are not responsible for their actions, yet I wonder if we have failed to recognize, understand, and believe that there is a spiritual war going on all around us.

Perhaps God's people in Daniel's time had come to believe that all their problems were simply the result of malicious national powers conquering the known world. After all, this small nation in the middle of Palestine had been a political football for a long time; since the Assyrians had conquered the northern ten tribes of Israel, the handwriting was on the wall for the southern tribes. In 586 B.C.,

Babylon conquered God's people and took them into exile; and by the time of Daniel 10, the Medes and Persians would conquer Babylon. And as we've already seen in Daniel 8, there would be more political and military machinations: Persia, Greece, the Seleucids, Rome. And in the midst of it all were God's people, fought over, exiled, taken away, brought here and there. If they weren't careful, God's people could come to believe that these political actors were actually the true forces in the world: it really was about Babylon v. Israel; Babylon v. Persia; Persia v. Greece; and so forth.

But if they thought that, they missed the point of what Daniel has been saying all through his book. Over and over again, Daniel has told us: trust in God. See him as the Lord of history, the King of time, the True King of the world, the one who is able to deliver from fiery furnaces and lions' dens. Nothing happens unless it is part of God's purpose and plan; he is the one who orders all things according to his glorious purpose. What we find in Daniel 10 is that this God, Daniel's God, lifts the veil a little bit to let us see that the battle is not an earthly one between nation states, kings and lords, or political parties. Rather, the real battle is one between spiritual forces: one against powers and principalities, cosmic powers over this present darkness, and the devil himself.

We can't fight this battle in our own strength or with our own resources. Rather, we need a faithful warrior who fights on our behalf and who will defeat our ancient foe. Only as we stand united to this great warrior will we be able to withstand in this evil day. Only as we trust in God as our faithful warrior will we see victory in the great war.

The Great War

In this chapter, right off the bat, we learn that the vision that Daniel saw was about a "great conflict" (10:1). This war was unlike the wars that had characterized the life of God's people to this point. After all, God's people were in exile as the result of a war. Nebuchadnezzar had fought against Judah, leveled Jerusalem, carted the best and brightest of the land back to Babylon. We can't sanitize what happened to Judah at the hands of the Babylonians: there was plundering, rape, desecration, destruction; there was slaughter and death, the killing of tens of thousands. And Babylon had engaged in warfare with Persia and had been utterly defeated as well. By the time of this vision, it was "the third year of Cyrus king of Persia" (10:1); the Medes and Persians had entered Babylon, killed Belshazzar and thousands beside, and established their rule.

And so, when Daniel heard about this vision of a great conflict and told his people about it, they might have thought automatically of the wars that they had known. But the war that this vision described was different. And the vision began with Daniel's time of fasting and mourning – a three-week period in which Daniel denied himself and sought God's face (10:2-3). God answered Daniel's plea by sending this "man clothed in linen" (10:5), who was clearly a supernatural being. The description given of this man suggested a dazzling figure whose body cast off a blue-green hue, whose face was shining resplendently, and whose voice was like a roaring crowd.

Daniel's response was to lose all his strength and to fall straight to the ground. But this supernatural being touched him and set him upright and spoke kind words: "O Daniel, man greatly loved, understand the words that I speak to you, and stand upright, for now I have been sent to you" (10:11). What comfort and courage Daniel must have felt: twice, he was told that he was a man "greatly loved" (10:11, 19), and three times, this supernatural being touched him (10:10, 16, 18). God clearly wanted to tell Daniel something vitally important, and so he encouraged him by word and touch to strengthen his heart.

Even more, Daniel should have taken courage from the fact that God had responded when he first started to fast and pray: "Fear not, Daniel, for from the first day that you set your heart to understand and humbled yourself before your God, your words have been heard, and I have come because of your words" (10:12). But there were larger spiritual forces at work: "The prince of the kingdom of Persia withstood me twenty-one days, but Michael, one of the chief princes, came to help me, for I was left there with the kings of Persia, and came to make you understand what is to happen to your people in the latter days. For the vision is for days yet to come" (10:13-14).

These verses suggest that the supernatural being had actually come in response to Daniel's prayer on the first day it was made; yet there was a larger spiritual battle, waged in places that Daniel could not see, that prevented his arrival for three weeks. Again, toward the end of the chapter in verses 20-21, the supernatural being says that he was returning to fight against "the prince of Persia" and that the "prince of Greece" will come. Further, there was none that contended by his side against these except "Michael, your prince."

Without going too far into what this may mean, I think we can say that the picture here was one of a cosmic battle – a battle waged by forces of evil against God's own powers. And the implication was that the scenes of Daniel 9, which promised the movements of Persia, Greece, and the four kingdoms, were not merely the actions of human actors, but reflected a larger reality beyond that which Daniel or God's people could see. And that larger reality, I want to suggest, is the real conflict in this world – a conflict between God's princes and a Warrior-to-come against "cosmic powers over this present darkness" (Eph. 6:12).

Now it is important to say that this perspective does not entail a dualistic worldview. It is not as though God and Satan are some equal deities, duking it out for world domination; nor are good and evil two great poles or balances in the life force that shape human destinies. No, God is the one who is over all; we've seen it over and over in Daniel's book. It is Yahweh who is the True King of the world, history, and time; there is nothing outside his control or purview. As Martin Luther apparently put it, our comfort comes from knowing that even the devil is God's devil.

But even though these forces of evil are somehow sub-servient to God and ultimately defeated by him, that doesn't mean that they aren't active and dangerous. We know texts such as 1 Peter 5:8, "Be sober-minded; be watchful. Your adversary the devil prowls around like a roaring lion, seek-ing someone to devour." If we were simply left to ourselves, to our own strength and ingenuity, as we resist the devil, we would be undone – because these spiritual forces are real and powerful and malignant. As Luther's familiar hymn puts it, "Did we in our own strength confide, our striving would be losing." What we need is someone who will fight on our behalf and who can defeat all our and his enemies.

Faithful warrior

That warrior has come. In fact, one of the key aspects of his war-making work was casting out demons, demonstra-ting his power as King over evil. Right at the beginning of Mark's Gospel, what was this Warrior doing? Con-fronting the man with the evil spirit, who had cried out in the middle of a worship service in Capernaum. The Warrior rebuked the spirit and said, "Be silent, and come out of him!" (Mark 1:23-26) And this Warrior noted that the work of casting out demons signaled something larger and better: "If it is by the Spirit of God that I cast out demons, then the Kingdom of God has come upon you" (Matt. 12:28). This Warrior was the coming King who has authority over the whole world.

And yet, this Warrior's greatest act in his holy war against the cosmic forces of evil looked like his greatest defeat. For he recognized that the central act in this holy war would be his willing submission to death on behalf of others. When he first told this to his followers, the voice of his enemy, Satan himself, was heard (Matt. 16:21-23). This Warrior knew that his great enemy wanted to kill him, and yet this Warrior knew that it was actually in dying that he would secure the salvation of the world. And so, as he went to the cross, this Warrior was not dissuaded. He knew that "now is the judgment of this world; now will the ruler of this world be cast out. And I, when I am lifted up from the earth, will draw all people to myself" (John 12:31-32).

And he was lifted up, suffering the cross, dying in the place of sinners, fully obedient to the will of his Father, bearing the wrath of God. It appeared that the serpent had not merely bruised the Warrior's heel, but had crushed him utterly. Until the third day — and then, the Warrior was alive, triumphant over death, receiving vindication from the Father, receiving the glory of God. And so it was that this Warrior had received a heel-bruise, but in his rising from the dead had crushed the serpent utterly.

Now who was this Warrior who disarmed these cosmic rulers and authorities and put them to open shame (Col. 2:15)? Who was this Warrior who in his dying and rising again has begun to destroy every rule and authority and power (1 Cor. 15:24)? Who has defeated ultimate evil and fear?

Who was this Warrior? This Warrior is Jesus our Lord. He is the one who fights on our side. He is the one who dispels the devil with a word. He is the one who stands as the mighty fortress of our God, the one to whom his people run. And as we put our whole-hearted faith in him, what we find is that his victory has become ours; his ultimate triumph belongs to us.

Continued warfare

Through our union with Jesus, the great and faithful Warrior, we are equipped to fight a true and continued warfare. That, of course, is the point of Ephesians 6:10-18: God has called upon us to "be strong in the Lord and in the strength of his might" as we face "the schemes of the devil." We are at war. We may not see it because we are trapped in our sensate world in which all we can see are the things that we can touch and all we believe comes from what we can see. But the fact remains that we are engaged in a spiritual battle with real spiritual enemies who hate us and who desire to destroy us. However, we do not engage in this warfare of the Christian life in our own strength. Rather, by virtue of our union with Jesus, we put on the "whole armor of God:" we have his truth and righteousness, God's peace and God-granted faith. We stand in God's salvation, trusting in God's Word and prayer.

The only way that we can stand in this continuing warfare, fighting an already defeated but not yet fully vanquished foe, is to remember that we belong body and soul to the Great Warrior, Jesus, who has already fought on our behalf at the cross and empty tomb and who won all that was required for our salvation. And at the last day, he will appear again to vanquish finally all our and his enemies.

Until then, we must remember that the real battle is not the battle of Election Day, not our national wars, not the war on terror. The real battle is the spiritual battle that John Bunyan depicted so well in his *Pilgrim's Progress*. Christian had just left the Palace Beautiful and the comfort of Discretion, Charity, Piety, and Prudence. Having descended a difficult hill, Christian was immediately confronted by

Apollyon, a hideous monster that stood for the real forces of evil in this real battle we fight.

Repeatedly, Apollyon attempted to convince Christian that he must return to the devil's service; repeatedly, Christian refused. Finally, Apollyon straddled the road and raged, "I am an enemy to this Prince, I hate his person, his laws, and people: I am come out on purpose to withstand thee ... Prepare thyself to die; for I swear by my infernal den, that thou shalt go no farther: here will I spill thy soul!" After a fierce battle that took the better part of the day, it appeared that Apollyon would destroy Christian. And just at that moment, Christian seized his sword, the Word of God, and cried,

> *"Rejoice not against me, O mine enemy: when I fall, I shall arise"* (Micah 7:8); *and with that gave him a deadly thrust, which made him give back, as one that had received his mortal wound. Christian perceiving that, made at him again, saying,* "Nay, in all these things we are more than conquerors, through Him that loved us" (Rom. 8:37). *And with that Apollyon spread forth his dragon wings, and sped him away, that Christian saw him no more.*

It was that last thrust that drove the enemy away. It wasn't somehow Christian's strength that finally did Apollyon in. What did he say? He spoke of the reality that as Christians, we are more than conquerors, not because of anything in ourselves, but because of him who loved us and gave himself for us. Our battle is fought through him who loved us. It is by virtue of our union with this Warrior who has already won that we have victory in the midst of the spiritual battle. That is how we must fight this very real warfare.

In the midst of the spiritual battles we daily fight — battles against temptation, depression and despair, relational conflict — we must be persuaded that we are not alone. There is a Warrior who has fought for us, who stands by our side, indeed who by his Spirit is within us. And so, God is calling us to run to him and say, "King Jesus, defeat your and my enemy in my life. As I wrestle with my sin, with my depression, with my despair, drive deep in my heart this glorious truth: King Jesus, you have already won. Do not let the enemy use these weapons in my life. Do not let the fiery darts of the enemy destroy me. Rather, grant the victory that you have already won. For I am persuaded that there is nothing that can separate me from your love – neither life nor death, angels nor darkness nor principalities, nor things present, nor things to come, nor height, nor depth, nor anything else in all creation. You are the God who loved me and gave himself for me. You are the faithful Warrior."

If we would call out to the Warrior to fight his real battle, the good news is this: he has struck the enemy with a mortal wound already. And he continues to fight on our behalf, ensuring that though we fall, we shall rise again both now and at the last day. Thanks be to God!

FOR FURTHER REFLECTION

1. Why is it that we fail to recognize the real spiritual battle in which we are engaged? Why is it easier to focus our "war" against forces we can see (other people) instead of the enemy we can't see (the devil)?

2. In what ways do you find yourself attempting to fight your spiritual battles in your own strength? How's that going for you?

3. How does the reality that we are already united to a Warrior who has triumphed over our enemy give us strength to fight day to day?

11
A Final Word: Learning to trust a God of hope

What if you could know the end of your life's story? How would that change your understanding of what is going on right now? Most of us, I think, have a great desire to know the end of the story. That was impressed on me when we got our first digital video recorder (DVR). As I was reading the directions in the user manual for setting the DVR up, I ran across these words in bold print: **"Notice, you cannot fast forward live TV."** That notice was stunning on two fronts: one, why would anyone think that you could fast forward live TV? And two, why would the satellite dish company feel the need to put that notice in the user manual? Can you imagine someone sitting at home, watching a sporting event, mashing the fast forward button on the DVR?

We wish we could do that, don't we? We wish we could take the DVR button and fast-forward to the end of our lives, because then we would know how the story ends, and then we would understand the twists and turns of our lives to that moment.

To change the image: for me, reading a mystery novel is really difficult. I usually skip ahead and read the final fifty pages or so; once I know how the novel finishes, it makes it easier to understand the twists and turns of the book (and much less stressful to boot!). But what if we could know the last several pages of life's story? How would it help us understand the twists and turns of our lives' stories?

That is something like the way these last two chapters of Daniel work. God's people were in exile, first under the power of Babylon and then under the power of Persia. By this time, several groups of people are beginning to return to Jerusalem under the oversight of Zerubbabel. And yet, as will become clear, they were returning to a land of conflict; it would take another twenty years to complete the temple. And others would arise who would oppose and persecute them – returning to the land would not solve all their problems.

But how would they view it all if they knew how the story would unfold? Even more, how would they view it if they knew that the world would be set to rights, that the wicked would finally be punished and the righteous be rewarded? What about for us? How would we look at our lives differently if we knew how the story unfolded and how the story would end? How would we look at difficulties with our health or the health of a loved one differently? How would we look at struggles with our marriages, our families, our children? How would it cause us to view a job loss differently or challenges to our retirement? If somehow we could fast forward and know the end of the story, how would it change the way we view today?

If we are tempted to despair, then the comfort we should take from Daniel 11-12 with all its twists and turns, with all of its strangeness, is this: God knows the end from the beginning; he is the Alpha and Omega; he knows the end of the story. We can trust this God because he tells us the end before it happens. And we can trust this God because he holds out hope, the hope of the resurrection, the hope of the world being set to rights again. Evil will be dealt with; the righteous will be brought to life again; there will be rest.

We need a scorecard: rulers

As most people come to know about me, I am a huge baseball fan. One of the things that I inevitably do when I go to the ballpark is buy a scorecard; after all, the old saying is true, "You can't tell the players without a scorecard." One time, disaster struck: my wife Sara and I were dating at the time and we went to a Greenville (South Carolina) Braves game. At the time, the Braves were the AA team for the major league Atlanta Braves. I had bought my scorecard and was keeping score when it began to rain. We ran for cover, but my scorecard was soaked. How could I keep score? How could I know what was going on? How could I know who was in the game?

This section of Daniel feels like we need a scorecard because there are so many players shuttling in and out of the action. In the fifty-eight verses of these two chapters, there is this King of the South, that King of the North; this King of the North, that King of the South. We would get confused if we didn't have a scorecard.

One thing that can help us here is to remember that this is prophecy; and yet much of this prophecy has already been realized. In many ways, this chapter fits together with chapters 2 and 7, and especially chapter 8 – over and over again, God tells his people through Daniel that he is the Lord of history and the King of time. And he demonstrates this by unfolding the way history will play out during the period of silence, beginning around 400 B.C. We've seen the basic framework before – Persia, Greece, and the four generals whom history has called the Successors, or the *Diadochi*. While Daniel 8 focused on the conflict between Persia and Greece, Daniel 11 unfolds the relationship between the four successors of Alexander, and especially between "the kingdom of the South," which was Egypt ruled by the Ptolemies, and "the kingdom of the North," which was the Middle East and included Palestine, ruled by the Seleucids.

If someone wanted to unpack the real historical actors here, he could consult a solid evangelical commentary. For my purposes, I want to point out a couple of things that had specific reference to God's people. First, it is important to recognize that the area where these two kingdoms butted against each other was "the glorious land" (11:16). The Ptolemies, who controlled Egypt, extended their sphere of influence nearly all the way to Damascus, which was about 135 miles north of Jerusalem. And so, when God's people returned to Palestine, as the prophet Jeremiah had declared would happen, they would continue to be right in the middle of world history. Their land, the beautiful land, the glorious land, would be contested ground. As Israel returned to the land, it may have felt as though God had forgotten them, left them prey to rulers and powers outside his and their control, continued to subject them to oppression and desolation. But by speaking of this in advance, God was telling his people that he knew what was going to happen to them; he was telling them that he was the King of the world and that nothing took him by surprise.

A second thing to notice here is that the story focuses on one "contemptible person" (11:21) who would rule the kingdom of the north. The section from 11:21-32 describes scenes that could well be attributed to the rule of Antiochus IV Epiphanes, who would turn against God's people and especially against God's worship: "Forces from him shall appear and profane the temple and fortress, and shall take away the regular burnt offering. And they shall set up the abomination that makes desolate" (11:31). As we mentioned before, this abomination was most likely a holy object associated with the worship of Zeus, placed in the temple, to which a pig was sacrificed. Antiochus was opposed by a group of men known to history as the Maccabees, to whom the text may make reference in 11:32. Again, this part of the prophecy was important to remind God's people that even when wicked men came and opposed God and his people, that didn't take God by surprise. By warning his people in advance, God desired for them to be "wise" and to help others to understand. But even if they faltered, God also said that there was a larger purpose in view – namely, the purification of God's own people.

A third thing to notice about this section is the description of an ultimately evil ruler, who appears in Daniel 11:36-45.

And the king shall do as he wills. He shall exalt himself and magnify himself above every god, and shall speak astonishing things against the God of gods. He shall prosper till the indignation is accomplished; for what is decreed shall be done. He shall pay no attention to the gods of his fathers, or to the one beloved by women. He shall not pay attention to any other god, for he shall magnify himself above all. He shall honor the god of fortresses instead of these. A god whom his fathers did not know he shall honor with gold and silver, with precious stones and costly gifts. He shall deal with the strongest fortresses with the help of a foreign god. Those who acknowledge him he shall load with honor. He shall make them rulers over many and shall divide the land for a price (11:36-39).

Who is this? Is this Antiochus IV? Is this some other future human ruler? Is this the final Antichrist? I don't think we can say for sure. One argument that it may continue to refer to Antiochus IV is that the nickname "Epiphanes," which literally means "the Shining One," was also a way of claiming that he was "the manifest god." He very much thought that he was divine, a god above every deity. Still, we don't know. What we can say is that even when this one comes – one who "shall speak astonishing things against the God of gods," one who "shall not pay attention to any other god, for he shall magnify himself above all" – that our God even knows about this one. This ruler will not take God by surprise; his times and rules are in God's hand.

Now, God knows all of this about cosmic powers. What does he know about our lives? What does he know about the movements of our days? If he knows the movements of the king of Persia and the king of Greece, the Ptolemies and the Seleucids, if he can tell God's people what will happen before it happens, what about our lives? Doesn't God know about our days, our struggles, our opposition? Doesn't he know that we in fact wrestle and doubt and fear? Our questions are met by the answer that our God is the God who rules over all things, who knows, and who controls all things by the power of his word. And yet that is not the final hope.

Because we have other questions: where is the justice? Where is the hope that evil will finally be punished and faith in God rewarded? Where is the promise that these rulers are not the ultimate realities, but that there is one who will set all things to rights? Where is the promise that the end of the story is one that is worth waiting for, one that is worth trusting God for?

We have a Savior: resurrection

Our final hope centers on the fact that God will set the world to rights again. And a major piece of that program is resurrection. What we find in Daniel 12:2-3 is the most explicit teaching in the Old Testament on the resurrection of the just and unjust. After a time of trouble, at the very end of the age, "many of those who sleep in the dust of the earth shall awake, some to everlasting life, and some to shame and everlasting contempt."

In other words, there is coming a day when the world will be set to rights again, when ultimate justice and ultimate blessing will be meted out. There is reason to hope. But the hope is not simply the fact of the resurrection – for some of us, resurrection is not good news. For some, they will be raised to everlasting contempt. Some will be raised to experience eternal shame, eternal judgment, eternal fire. There is a day coming in which God will judge the world; he will separate the sheep from the goats, the wheat from the tares, the good fish from the bad, those who love Christ from those who do not. And this promised Day of Judgment is part of what God is doing when he sets the world to rights.

Isaiah 65:17-25 presents a glorious picture of the new heavens and new earth. But what precedes that description of new heavens and new earth is a dark description of judgment. When God comes to visit the world in the final Day of the Lord, it is a day of both salvation and judgment. Resurrection is a resurrection to salvation and judgment.

And so, if we are not followers of Jesus Christ, the fact that there is going to be a resurrection and a time of ultimate judgment is very bad news. Because the day is coming when all unbelievers will be judged by God against the standard of his perfect righteousness and holiness, which is summed up in his moral law and especially in the Ten Commandments. If we face that judgment with only our good works and good thoughts and good intentions, and not with perfect works, thoughts, and intentions, then God's response – made plain throughout the Bible – is judgment.

One place among many in the Bible where this is made plain is 2 Thessalonians 1:7-10, where Paul tells us that Jesus is coming with

> *his mighty angels in flaming fire, inflicting vengeance on those who do not know God and on those who do not obey the gospel of our Lord Jesus. They will suffer the punishment of eternal destruction, away from the presence of the Lord and from the glory of his might, when he comes on that day to be glorified in his saints, and to be marveled at among all who have believed, because our testimony to you was believed.*

Here's what we should hear from this text: hell is real. Judgment is certain. Our only hope comes from having "obeyed the gospel of our Lord Jesus," which is nothing less and nothing more than, "Believe in the Lord Jesus, and you will be saved" (Acts 16:31).

It may very well be that God is shouting through the circumstances of life to stop trusting in our performance and to receive Jesus Christ as Lord and Savior. What does that mean? It means recognizing that Jesus came to live with perfect works, thoughts, and intentions, not for himself, but for others. And he came to die to satisfy God's wrath against sin, but not for his own sin, but others'. Those who come pleading Jesus' blood and righteousness, resting in Jesus' finished work instead of his or her own imperfect works, will find a full and free salvation.

And this salvation includes a resurrection to everlasting life where we "shall shine like the brightness of the sky above" (12:3). We will participate both now and then in God's work of redemption and renewal, in God's work of making all things new. This is the great hope – that our faithful God, who is the True King, the faithful King, the King who is able to save, the King who is merciful – that this God has come near to us in Jesus to save us. And this Jesus is the Resurrection and the Life; those who trust in this Savior are those who have hope both in this life and the life to come.

We look for salvation: rest

Trusting in this Jesus, the Resurrection and the Life, gives us rest. And that is exactly what the angels tell Daniel to do. Right at the end of the prophecies of his book, the passage reads: "But go your way till the end. And you shall rest and shall stand in your allotted place until the end of the days" (12:9). Rest in the promises of God, in the promise of who God is and what God has done in his mighty acts and words of salvation.

But it is hard for us to rest, especially when our questions remain unanswered. Daniel still had unanswered questions: "O my lord, what shall be the outcome of these things?" (12:8). But this man who received so many answers through visions and victories was told, "Go your way, Daniel" (12:9). Go your way, you shall rest, you must rest. Indeed, the numbers that appear throughout this book, and even in this last chapter, force us to trust in God and to rest in his provision: time, times, and half a time; 1,290 days; 1,335 days; seventy weeks. How do they all work together? We don't know, but we do know that God alone knows – he has determined the end from the beginning, and we can trust in him.

And yet, we confess that it is hard to rest when our questions about our lives don't get answered. We would love to be able to take those DVR buttons and hit the fast forward, but we can't. And so, we know the end of the story – resurrection, salvation, judgment – and we know that God knows all the movements of the story in which we live. In the meantime, we continue to hope in this God, to rest in him, to trust him.

As we live as exiles in this world, away from our true country and our true home, we learn that the gods of this world, the rulers of this world, are no gods and no rulers. We learn that there is only one True King, who is the God of Israel and the church, who has come near to us in Jesus Christ and by his Spirit. We learn to trust in him as our true hero, to rest and to sing with whole-hearted faith:

> *Crown him the Lord of years, the Potentate of time;*
> *Creator of the rolling spheres, ineffably sublime;*
> *All hail, Redeemer, hail! For thou hast died for me:*
> *Thy praise shall never, never fail throughout eternity.*

FOR FURTHER REFLECTION

1. How does knowing the end of the salvation story make dealing with our pain and suffering now more bearable?

2. For some, resurrection is not good news but bad news, because it is resurrection to eternal judgment. Consider how God's work in the last day involves <u>both</u> salvation and judgment.

3. Here at the end of Daniel, it's helpful to consider what you've learned. What are three things that God has shown you about himself through this study?

Notes on Sources

CHAPTER 1
The Andrew Jackson quote came from Robert V. Remini: *Andrew Jackson*, 3 vols. (Baltimore: Johns Hopkins University Press, 1998), 1:1. William Cowper's hymn is "God Moves in a Mysterious Way," *Trinity Hymnal* (Suwanee, GA: Great Commission Publications, 1991), #128.

CHAPTER 2
William Williams, "Guide Me, O Thou Great Jehovah," *Trinity Hymnal* (Suwanee, GA: Great Commission Publications, 1991), #598.

CHAPTER 3
The version of the Heidelberg Catechism cited comes from the Christian Reformed Church of North America: http://www.crcna.org/pages/ heidelberg_intro.cfm. The John Newton hymn text, "I asked the Lord that I might grow," can be found here: http://www.cyberhymnal.org/ htm/i/a/iaskedtl.htm. The final hymn text comes from "How Firm a Foundation," *Trinity Hymnal* (Suwanee, GA: Great Commission Publications, 1991), #94.

CHAPTER 4
The account of the Ali-Liston fight summarizes the information found at http://en.wikipedia.org/wiki/Muhammad_Ali_vs._Sonny_Liston. The video of the fight's final rounds can be found on YouTube here: http://youtu.be/58AzC4wAhgI. Samuel Rodigast, "Whate'er My God Ordains is Right," *Trinity Hymnal* (Suwanee, GA: Great Commission Publications, 1991), #108.

CHAPTER 5

The Patrick story came from Ted Olsen, *Christianity and the Celts* (Downers Grove: InterVarsity, 2003), 71-2. The Toby Keith line is from the song "Beer for My Horses," from *Unleashed* (SKG Music Nashville, 2002). The story of George W. Bush after 9/11 came from *Decision Points* (New York: Crown, 2011), 148. The hymn, "How Deep the Father's Love for Us," is by Stuart Townend, whose website can be found at http://www.stuarttownend.co.uk/. The phrase "o'er every foe victorious" comes from the final verse of "Hail to the Lord's Anointed," *Trinity Hymnal* (Suwanee, GA: Great Commission Publications, 1991), #311.

CHAPTER 6

The account of the martyrdom of Ignatius comes from *Early Christian Writings: The Apostolic Fathers* (New York: Penguin, 1987), 113-36. The story of Robert Bruce is found in Iain Murray, *A Scottish Christian Heritage* (Carlisle, PA: Banner of Truth, 2006), 58.

CHAPTER 7

The quote from the 1873 PCUSA General Assembly comes from Sean Michael Lucas, *Robert Lewis Dabney: A Southern Presbyterian Life* (Phillipsburg, NJ: P&R, 2005), 153. The account of James Guthrie can be found in Jock Purves, *Fair Sunshine: Character Studies of the Scottish Covenanters* (Carlisle, PA: Banner of Truth, 1968), 13-21 (the quote is on p. 16).

CHAPTER 8

An account of the Millerites can be found in David L. Rowe, *God's Strange Work: William Miller and the End of the World* (Grand Rapids: Eerdmans, 2008). My summary of ancient Near Eastern history can be found in any standard evangelical commentary; I followed Tremper Longman, III, *Daniel*, NIV Application Commentary (Grand Rapids: Zondervan, 1999). The quotation of the Heidelberg Catechism came from http://www.crcna.org/pages/heidelberg_intro.cfm.

Notes on Sources

CHAPTER 9

The summary of the fast day activities of the Civil War armies came from Harry S. Stout, *Upon the Altar of the Nation: A Moral History of the Civil War* (New York: Viking, 2006). Abraham Lincoln's Second Inaugural Address can be found in many places on the Internet; one such place is here: http://www.loc.gov/rr/program/bib/ourdocs/ Lincoln2nd.html. My discussion of New England Puritans and the national covenant refers to Ernest Lee Tuveson, *Redeemer Nation: The Idea of America's Millennial Role* (Chicago: University of Chicago Press, 1980). I used lines from Horatius Bonar's hymn, "Thy Works, Not Mine, O Christ," *Trinity Hymnal* (Suwanee, GA: Great Commission Publications, 1991), #524. The story from Rose Marie Miller is found in her book, *From Fear to Freedom: Living as Sons and Daughters of God* (Wheaton, IL: Shaw Books, 2000).

CHAPTER 10

Pat Buchanan's "culture war" speech can be found on the Internet here: http://web.archive.org/web/20071018035401/http://www.buchanan. org/pa-92-0817-rnc.html. The book that Buchanan drew from was James Davison Hunter, *Culture Wars: The Struggle to Control the Family, Art, Education, Law, and Politics in America* (New York: Basic, 1992). The account of Christian and Apollyon can be found in any version of Bunyan's *Pilgrim's Progress*; one is John Bunyan, *Pilgrim's Progress* (Fearn, Ross-shire, UK: Christian Focus, 2005), 65-66.

CHAPTER 11

Matthew Bridges, "Crown Him with Many Crowns," *Trinity Hymnal* (Suwanee, GA: Great Commission Publications, 1991), #295.

Liam Goligher

This practical, Christ-centered exposition of the Joseph narrative celebrates the good sovereignty of God, who shapes our lives for his service. **PHILIP G. RYKEN**

Joseph
The Hidden hand of God

ISBN 978-1-84550-368-0

Joseph
The Hidden Hand of God
LIAM GOLIGHER

Taking care to retell Joseph's story as originally set out by the divine author, this book is a gripping read. But, of course, it is so much more than that. It is very encouraging to read from his real-life drama, how God achieved his purpose by using members of a highly dysfunctional family... This book is easily accessible to someone with little or no biblical knowledge, and is also stimulating to others who have travelled this way many times before.

Evangelicals Now

Liam Goligher is a gifted communicator with a passion for God's Word, including the stories of the Old Testament. This practical, Christ-centered exposition of the Joseph narrative celebrates the good sovereignty of God, who shapes our lives for his service.

Philip G. Ryken,
President, Wheaton College, Wheaton, Illinois

The story of Joseph is a great symphony on the theme of God's providence. But a symphony can only be brought to life by a skilled expert who understands and can interpret all the nuances of the music. Enter Liam Goligher and we know the music is in safe hands. In his hands the Joseph Symphony intrigues, delights, and captivates our hearts for God and his ways and fills us with admiration for his wise providence. Here is a book to put melody into the way we live the Christian life.

Sinclair B. Ferguson,
Senior Minister, First Presbyterian Church, Columbia, South Carolina

Liam Goligher is Senior Minister of Tenth Presbyterian Church, Philadelphia, Pennsylvania

Christian Focus Publications
publishes books for all ages

Our mission statement –

STAYING FAITHFUL
In dependence upon God we seek to impact the world through literature faithful to His infallible Word, the Bible. Our aim is to ensure that the Lord Jesus Christ is presented as the only hope to obtain forgiveness of sin, live a useful life and look forward to heaven with Him.

REACHING OUT
Christ's last command requires us to reach out to our world with His gospel. We seek to help fulfil that by publishing books that point people towards Jesus and help them develop a Christ-like maturity. We aim to equip all levels of readers for life, work, ministry and mission.

Books in our adult range are published in three imprints:

Christian Focus contains popular works including biographies, commentaries, basic doctrine and Christian living. Our children's books are also published in this imprint.

Mentor focuses on books written at a level suitable for Bible College and seminary students, pastors, and other serious readers. The imprint includes commentaries, doctrinal studies, examination of current issues and church history.

Christian Heritage contains classic writings from the past.

Christian Focus Publications Ltd,
Geanies House, Fearn, Ross-shire,
IV20 1TW, Scotland, United Kingdom.
www.christianfocus.com